365 Incredible Animals

365
Incredible
Animals

Laure Maj

FIREFLY BOOKS

A FIREFLY BOOK

Published by Firefly Books Ltd. 2016

Original French title (365 Animaux Encroyables) copyright © 2015
EDITIONS PLAYBAC / PRISMA PRESS / GEO.
33 rue du Petit Musc, 75004, Paris. France
This English edition copyright © 2016 Firefly Books

First printing

Publisher Cataloging-in-Publication Data (U.S.)

A CIP record for this title is available from the Library of Congress

Library and Archives Canada Cataloguing in Publication

A CIP record for this title is available from Library and Archives
Canada

Published in the United States by
Firefly Books (U.S.) Inc.
P.O. Box 1338, Ellicott Station
Buffalo, New York 14205

Published in Canada by
Firefly Books Ltd.
50 Staples Avenue, Unit 1
Richmond Hill, Ontario L4B 0A7

Translation: Claudine Mercereau

Printed in China

The Male Frigatebird: A Real Ladies' Bird

The male frigatebird, a large ocean-going bird of the tropics, inflates the enormous red pouch under its throat to seduce females. During this display, its pouch can remain inflated for over 20 minutes!

5

Dancing Seals

Two female seals brush up against one another, swimming side by side. They play together gracefully to seduce the only male who leads the group. These aquatic choreographies are mostly visible during mating season, in September.

A Young Panther to Protect

The female panther must feed her young, but she must also find them hiding spots. When she leaves them to hunt, they can become prey for lions, hyenas and even other adult panthers, which don't hesitate to kill their future rivals.

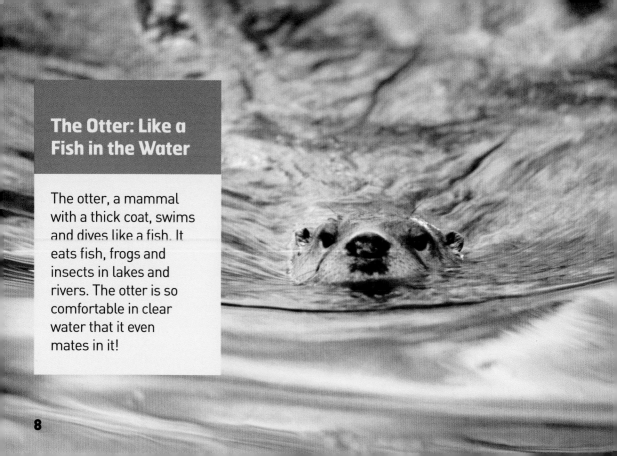

The Otter: Like a Fish in the Water

The otter, a mammal with a thick coat, swims and dives like a fish. It eats fish, frogs and insects in lakes and rivers. The otter is so comfortable in clear water that it even mates in it!

Solidarity Is Vital for Penguins

Without huddling against each other to keep warm, penguins would not survive Antarctic storms. The birds on the outside of the group are more exposed to the wind than those in the center, so they regularly exchange positions.

The Shire Horse: A Gentle Giant

Calm and docile, the Shire horse is easy to train. It is also the biggest and heaviest horse in the world. Due to its strength, it is often used in horse teams or to work fields. They are also ridden for leisure and in shows. Elegant and muscular, the Shire horse has a fine figure.

A Harlequin Crab Seeks Refuge Under a Sea Anemone

The sea anemone is an animal that, like the jellyfish, has tentacles with tiny pockets full of poison that it projects with harpoon-like appendages. Predators without shells won't attack this crab for fear of rubbing up against the anemone and its venomous arms.

The Panther Chameleon Hunts by Keeping Still

The panther chameleon is endemic to the island of Madagascar. Its eyes allow it to see in all directions while sitting still. That's how it spots insects; it then catches them by deploying its long, sticky tongue.

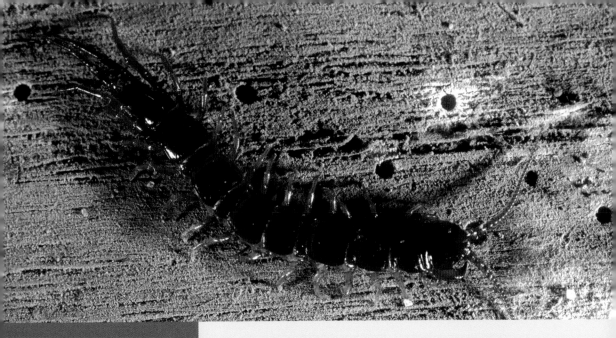

Centipedes Move Slowly

The body of the centipede is made up of different parts with articulations between them, and each part has one or two pairs of legs, depending on the species. The centipede uses its long legs to move with its characteristic slow undulations.

What Is this Kingfisher Spitting Out?

This kingfisher is spitting out a ball of scales and fish bones that it can't digest. Other birds, like the owl, use this same technique, and so do some mammals. Similarly, cats often spit out balls that are mostly made of hair that they've swallowed while licking themselves.

The Groundhog Stands Guard

While the other members of the colony graze, this groundhog looks up at the sky, from where eagles can attack, as well as the horizon, from where lynx or stray dogs may appear. When threatened, it whistles a warning, and the entire troop disappears into their burrows.

The White Rhinoceros Is Actually Gray!

Where does the name white rhinoceros come from? South Africans of Dutch heritage called it "wijd-lip" (wide lips) because of its wide snout, but the English heard "white," and the name stuck.

The Blenny Fiercely Defends Its Territory

The blenny is a strange fish with an elongated body but no scales. It often hides and will lift its head out of its shelter, leaning on transparent fins that act like elbows. It may be small but it has character, and it doesn't hesitate to intimidate fish that are much bigger than it.

The Coconut Crab Adores Coconuts

The coconut crab, found on the shores of the Indian and Pacific Oceans, sometimes climbs up coconut trees to pick the nuts with its claws. It also eats fruit, fish and crab carcasses, which it finds with the help of its excellent sense of smell.

The Spotted Hyena's Tremendous Jaws

The spotted hyena's jaws are so powerful that they can crush the biggest and hardest bones. Thanks to them, hyenas play an important role in maintaining the ecological balance of the African savanna. They eat animal carcasses, thereby preventing diseases from spreading.

What Is this Emu Looking For?

Fat and muscular, this cousin of the ostrich doesn't like leaves or grass. It prefers rich vegetation, such as seeds, fruit and shoots, or animals, such insects, lizards and small rodents. To find them, the emu travels long distances. It also swallows small stones to help its stomach break down food.

A Green Lizard Comes out of Hiding

During the summer, we often see green lizards in warm and sun-exposed areas. They eat insects, including earthworms, and, more rarely, chicks and fruit. When winter hits these lizards disappear, hibernating under tree trunks or in rodent burrows.

The Crinoid: Plant or Animal?

Often called the "sea lily," the crinoid is actually an animal! Its mouth is on its central disk. Spikes on the other side of the disk serve as feet. Its numerous filamentous "arms" allow it to capture plankton and bring it to its mouth to eat.

The Leaf Beetle: An Insect Among Millions

This insect is one of the numerous parasites of the tropical and equatorial forests. These forests are inhabited by millions of insects, many of which are still unknown. There are more than 10 million species yet to be discovered on our planet!

The Cheetah: A Feline in Danger

It is estimated that there were 100,000 cheetahs a century ago. Today, there are less than 10,000. In Africa, they can only be found in sanctuaries, and they have mostly disappeared from Asia as well. Why such a decline in their population? Their territory has been gradually taken over by humans, and their population has been decimated by hunting.

Why Does the Buff-Tailed Bumblebee Have Hairs?

The hairs that cover the buff-tailed bumblebee make it a champion pollinator. When this insect penetrates a flower, its hairs catch a large quantity of pollen. When it moves on to another flower, the pollen is spread to that flower. Hence, the reproduction of the planet is ensured.

The Wolf's Fascinaing Eyes

Blue at birth, the wolf's eyes become amber yellow by adult age. Their eyes are covered in silvery platelets that capture and reflect the light, making them phosphorescent. This gives the animal excellent vision in low light — and even allows them to see at night.

The Mudskipper: A Fish on Guard

Living in tropics and as much in water as on sand, the mudskipper doesn't like sharing its territory. If another mudskipper wanders in, it raises its dorsal fins and opens its mouth wide. This usually suffices to make the intruder leave.

The Mother Seal Never Loses Her Baby

During the first two weeks of a seal pup's life, its mother doesn't leave its side. She then returns to the sea to eat, leaving her newborn on the shore with the other little ones. When she comes back to nurse her pup, she recognizes it among all the others by its smell.

The Siamese Fighting Fish's Love Nest

To mate, these fish create a nest made of bubbles. The male then interlaces the female and discharges his semen on her eggs as she's laying them. Afterward, the male chases the female away from the nest and guards the eggs from intruders. One day later, the eggs hatch.

The Desman Has a Good Nose

The desman lives along the shores of torrents in the Pyrenees Mountains. It spends the majority of its time looking for insects, larvae and fish eggs. To do this, it digs along the bottom of the water with its snout. Its nose compensates for its poor vision, and it can use it as a shovel, nose and radar all in one.

The Gorilla: A Giant on a Diet

The gorilla of the West African plains has a very healthy diet: fruit during the rainy season and leaves and bark the rest of the year with some termites and other insects thrown in. Yet he looks like an ogre: the male measures just over 5 feet (1.6 m) and weighs, on average, almost 450 pounds (200 kg)!

The Azure Damselfly's Synchronized Swimming

These damselflies mate in an unusual way: the male catches the female with the end of his abdomen, and the female curves her abdomen toward him to be impregnated. Then the male stays attached while the female deposits her eggs on the surface of the water.

The Majestic African Buffalo

The African buffalo is the tallest and heaviest of all the African bovines. They are as tall as a man and can weigh more than 1 ton (0.9 metric tons)! When they are attacked, they form a circle to protect their young. Positioned in such a way, with their horns in front of them, they are almost invincible.

The Multicolored Poison Dart Frog

This frog's bright colors warn predators that its skin is very venomous. The indigenous people of Costa Rica use the venom of this tiny amphibian to poison their arrowheads.

The Noisy Great Hornbill

As its name suggests, the great hornbill is a noisy bird. It toots, barks and howls from the top of the highest tree branches, where it lives in South-East Asian tropical forests. When it's flying, the beating of its big wings also makes a particular noise.

35

The Paper Wasp's Nest

The mandible (or jaw) of this wasp is very powerful. With it, the wasps can knead wood fibers and transform them into a ball. They use this ball of papier-mâché to build their nest, which will house a small swarm of around 20 wasps.

The White-Headed Capuchin Lives in the Trees

The white-headed capuchin feeds on insects, fruit, nuts, seeds and invertebrates. Like many other animals of South American tropical forests, this little monkey is arboreal: it lives in trees and only comes down to drink. By doing so, it avoids attacks by snakes and other terrestrial predators.

A Polar Bear
Cub's Beginnings

Female polar bears give birth every three years. The first few months after giving birth, the cubs stay with their mother in her den. When the entire family emerges, usually at the beginning of March, the mother must be very vigilant, since wolves and other bears will hunt her cubs without pity.

The American Alligator Is a Real Charmer!

American alligators live in freshwater and marshes of the southeast United States. During mating season, the male uses every trick he can think of to please the female. He pats her on the legs, rubs up against her throat and even blows bubbles on her snout. If he seduces her, they will mate in the water.

The Sheep of New Zealand

There are almost 50 million sheep in New Zealand, which means the country has 13 times more sheep than people! They are raised for their meat but also for their wool, which differs according to their breed. The wool is used to create rugs, carpets and sweaters.

Tigers Love to Swim

Tigers happily dive in lakes and waterways to refresh themselves but also to get rid of the insects and parasites lodged in their thick fur. Being excellent swimmers, they can cover many miles. Their baths are usually followed by a long nap.

The Blue-and-Yellow Macaw: A Parrot in Danger

The blue-and-yellow macaw lives in the tropical forests of Central America. Its predators are big birds of prey such as harpy eagles and hawk eagles. However, the biggest threat to this bird is humans, who are destroying their forest habitat and, even though it's illegal, capturing them to sell in the pet trade.

The Madagascar Boa's Sixth Sense

Like all snakes, the Madagascar boa has two holes in the roof of its mouth in addition to its nostrils. They move their forked tongue to capture fragrant particles that they then bring into their two orifices, which is how they gather additional information about their environment.

The Steller's Jay Is Beautiful but Not Timid

Nature lovers and campers in America's West can easily observe this beautiful blue jay. It eats seeds, pinecones, insects and fruit, and it isn't afraid to approach people to see if they have food it can steal.

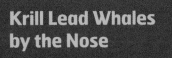

Krill Lead Whales by the Nose

Krill are a variety of planktonic crustacean composed primarily of different species of small, transparent shrimp. They are the favorite meal of whales, which swallow many tons per day! Thus, the movement of these crustaceans affects the migration of these giants of the sea.

45

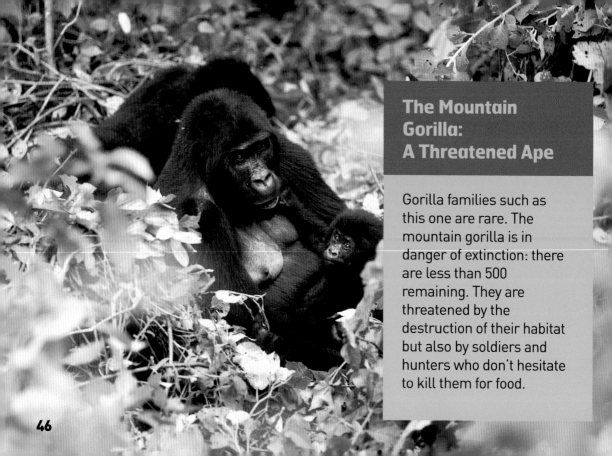

The Mountain Gorilla: A Threatened Ape

Gorilla families such as this one are rare. The mountain gorilla is in danger of extinction: there are less than 500 remaining. They are threatened by the destruction of their habitat but also by soldiers and hunters who don't hesitate to kill them for food.

The Sand Cat's Attack

Adapted to life in the desert, this cat almost never drinks and can survive by absorbing water from the animals it eats. Thanks to its very good hearing, it can locate prey over long distances. The sand cat's color allows it to move unnoticed and surprise its prey, like this viper that's about to be attacked.

The Green Heron's Unexpected Colors

The green heron can also be gray or red! It is found in numerous areas around the world, and its plumage changes color from one region to the next. It is small compared to other herons: it measures under 10 inches (25 cm) from the top of its head to the end of its feet.

The Pill Millipede's Weapons

This millipede has two means of defense. When a predator approaches or touches it, it rolls its shell up, taking the shape of a small, solid marble. The pill millipede is also armed with glands that release a repulsive odor, which acts as an appetite suppresant for anything that might want to eat it.

Camouflage

Animals have a thousand and one ways to hide themselves. This fish is concealing itself in sand, leaving only one eye showing. Other animals take on the color of their surroundings, and certain animals imitate plants or a part of a bigger animal. All of these camouflage methods have the same goal: to deceive so the animal can surprise its prey or avoid its predators.

The Brown Bear Is a Good Climber

Thanks to its powerful claws, the brown bear can climb up tree trunks and seek refuge when it senses danger. It also climbs to find food. It is an omnivore, so it eats a bit of everything: leaves, plants, berries and other fruits, insects, fish and small mammals.

The Eurasian Blue Tit: An Acrobatic Bird

To reach the hole in the tree in which it nests, the blue tit becomes a bit of an acrobat, by putting its feet out front of it. Sometimes it also balances itself on thin branches to catch a caterpillar or a seed with its robust beak.

Nutrias Have Invaded Europe

Originally from South America, nutrias, also called coypus, were imported to Europe for the fur trade. Some escaped from their breeding farms and spread throughout the continent. Their burrows, dug on the edge of ponds or rivers, can cause the collapse of riverbanks.

The Cape Ground Squirrel: A Happy Companion

This sociable squirrel from South Africa usually lives in colonies of six to ten individuals and has a playful personality. It is called a "ground" squirrel because, with the help of its solid claws, it digs in the ground in search of seeds and roots.

The Snow Leopard: Victim of Its Beauty

This male leopard has caught a female by the neck, but he won't kill her. The real danger is the humans who hunt these felines for their superb fur. Unless drastic measures are taken, the snow leopard will soon disappear from the mountains of Central Asia.

The Swallowtail Butterfly's Wings

The swallowtail's colored wings, like those of all butterflies, are made of flattened scales arranged like shingles on a roof. A butterfly's scales vary in size and number; certain species have more than 1 million. These scales can easily fall off when the butterfly flies or when it is caught.

The Bat's Double Life

In flight, this bat appears bigger than it really is: its wingspan is just under 9 inches (22 cm). But when it's in its usual resting position, suspended upside down, it looks very small. It weighs less than ¼ ounce (10 g).

On the Jaguar's Trail

A jaguar has been here and has left some tracks in the moist dirt. They are those of its back paws, which only have four digits; its front paws have five. Its claws don't appear because they're retractable. They only come out when the jaguar attacks, fights or climbs trees.

Mother Crocodiles Protect Their Young

Female crocodiles can delicately move their babies from the nest to the water. Without their mother, hatchlings, which measure less than 10 inches (25 cm), would be ideal prey. As an adult, they will be strong reptiles measuring over 13 feet (4 m) long and will be almost invincible.

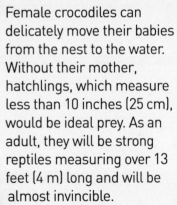

Jellyfish See Nothing and Hear Nothing!

The jellyfish is an unusual animal, with its gelatinous umbrella and many tentacles. It is not able to see or smell, but the sensors on its umbrella allow it to detect the movements that predators and other animals make in the water.

American White Pelicans Are Clever Fishers

American white pelicans fish in a group, stuck one against the other, and push the fish toward the shore. Once they have trapped their prey, they capture them in the sack under their bill before swallowing them. When it is warm, this sack also serves to lower their body temperature.

The Snail Is One of the Hedgehog's Favorite Meals

The hedgehog adores mollusks, slugs and snails but also centipedes and caterpillars. It won't complain about worms, frogs or chicks either. It eats a bit of everything and helps gardeners rid themselves of animals that steal their vegetables.

The Pangolin's Scaled Armor

Only the belly of the pangolin isn't covered with scales. When threatened, it protects its belly by rolling onto itself, its head down between its front legs. The pangolin is careful and prefers to feed at night. It captures its prey with its long tongue covered with sticky saliva.

This Majestic Blue Peacock Is Spreading Its Tail

The blue peacock deploys its long train of feathers, which can measure more than 5 feet (1.6 m), both to intimidate potential predators and to attract females. The peacock has been domesticated for almost 2,000 years. It's prized for the beauty of its plumage, with its brilliant blue eyespots, as well as for its abilities as a watchman — it has a very loud scream.

The Small Emperor Moth's Optical Illusion

The eyespots on the wings of this moth trick and frighten potential predators, who think they see a beast with big eyes. Its comb-like antennae are equally stunning; those of butterflies are, by contrast, very thin.

Chimpanzees Are Big Talkers

Chimpanzees communicate with each other using numerous sounds but also with facial expressions, movements, postures and by touch. Sounds and mimicry allow them to express a range of emotions.

66

Beware the Crocodile Camouflaged Among the Lily Pads

Crocodiles are formidable hunters. They hide in watering places then, using their powerful back legs, leap on their prey as it's quenching its thirst. It's not a big deal if it misses its target, however; crocodiles can survive for many months without eating a single bite.

Raccoons Are Fastidious Cleaners

Raccoons clean their food before eating it. Imported to Europe for their fur, some of these American mammals escaped, and the species is now pervasive in wooded areas near lakes and rivers throughout Europe and Asia.

Is this Ghost Crab Winking?

The ghost crab got its name due to its pale yellow color, which allows it to blend in with the sand and surprise — as would a ghost — other animals wandering around at night. Its eyes are located at the end of a small arm that it can lift to better see around it. The male uses its big claw as a weapon to defend its territory.

How Barbary Macaques Keep Warm

These females and this young macaque are keeping each other warm. These monkeys can withstand big variations in temperatures thanks to their fur, which is short in the summer and long and lush in the winter. They live in groups, and the relationships between females (mothers, grandmothers, sisters) are particularly well developed.

The Beautiful Keel-Billed Toucan

Due to its unique and superbly colored bill, it's difficult to mistake this toucan for any other bird! It uses its bill to reach fruit in branches too fragile to support its weight. It also uses its bill to chase away other toucans that try to appropriate its nest.

This Butterfly Is an Apollo

This big Apollo lives at an altitude of up to 8,200 feet (2,500 m) in the Alps as well as in Finland and Sweden. It is one of the largest European butterflies, with an average wingspan of just under 3 inches (7 cm). It's a protected species that likes to warm itself in the sun, on flowers and on rocks.

The Koala: A True Australian

Like many islands, Australia is home to many endemic species of animals: the seas and oceans that surround it have kept them isolated. This is the case for the koala, a small marsupial with the appearance of a stuffed animal, which lives in the eucalyptus forests of eastern Australia. It eats leaves exclusively from this tree.

The Seahorse: Champion of Camouflage

Too slow to escape, the only chance seahorses have to save their eggs from predators is to avoid being seen. Their skin perfectly imitates the seaweed in which they like to hide.

Female Chamois Live Together

In the spring, a female chamois isolates herself to give birth. She then regroups, along with her young, with the other females, but they remain separated from the males. It's only at the end of the year that everyone is reunited to spend the winter together.

The Weasel Is a Farmer's Friend

When weasels are around, it's disastrous for small rodents that destroy crops. These small carnivores are fond of rodents and are a particularly efficient predator. Their senses of smell and hearing allow them to locate field mice and voles day or night.

The Frog's Sad Destiny

Frog numbers are decreasing little by little. The destruction of the wetlands where they live, the effects of water pollution, highway expansion and increased car traffic are decimating their population.

The Arctic Fox: A Hunter White as Snow

The fur that covers the Arctic fox's body — even under its paws — allows it to withstand extreme cold. During the winter, its white coat helps to camouflage it from its prey, such as seal cubs. However, this clever fox can also content itself with a meal made up of a polar bear's leftovers.

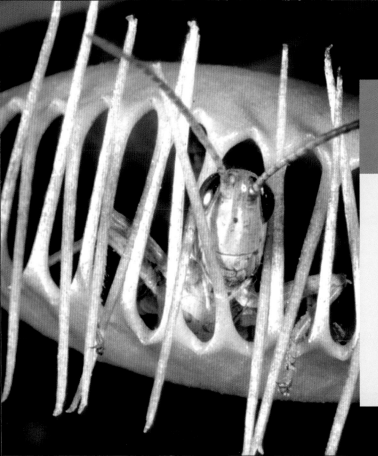

This Carnivorous Plant Is Keeping a Cricket Prisoner

This cricket landed on a Venus flytrap, attracted to the substances it creates. The plant detected its presence right away, via the sensitive cilium under its two lobes, and it shut these lobes tight in less than a fraction of a second. The insect, now trapped, will be slowly "digested" by the plant.

The Great Egret Makes Its Nest

This egret nests in reed beds or in trees on the edges of lakes and ponds. It makes its nest of dry reeds and plants it finds in marshes. Between April and June, the female lays three to five eggs and incubates them for almost a month. The chicks won't fly away until a month and a half after they hatch.

This Small Gecko Has a Big Lick

In the vast desert of Namibia, Africa, it is very cold at night. The water in the air condenses on rocks, plants and even animals, which forms dew. With one lick, the gecko can retrieve the small droplets that have accumulated on its body and drink them.

Wolverines Don't Share

The membranes that join the wolverine's fingers and large feet allow it to walk on snow without sinking. It's very territorial and solitary, and it will keep intruders away. It is a cousin of the beech marten and is found in North America, Europe and Asia.

The Common Redshank: A Strange Wader

The common redshank's long legs are perfect for walking in marshes, estuaries and on the edges of ponds. It eats by pecking worms, insects, mollusks and crustaceans. When threatened, it uses its very loud piping call to warn other waders.

The Jaguar's Impressive Fangs

When they feel threatened, jaguars growl and snarl. Their remarkably well-developed senses of hearing and smell allow them to quickly detect intruders in the lush tropical forest of South America, where they live. Once they've scared off the nuisance, these felines can return to their favorite pastime — sleeping!

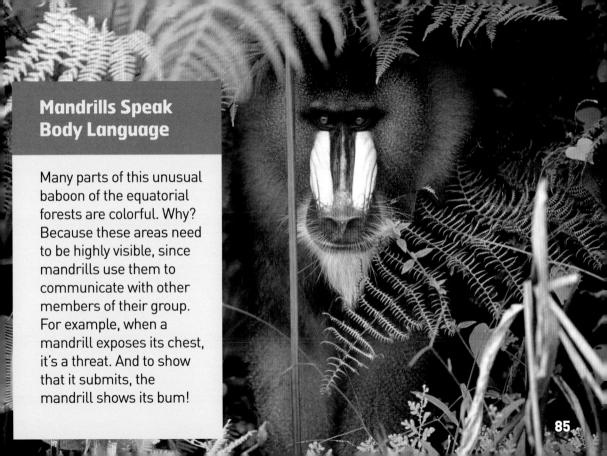

Mandrills Speak Body Language

Many parts of this unusual baboon of the equatorial forests are colorful. Why? Because these areas need to be highly visible, since mandrills use them to communicate with other members of their group. For example, when a mandrill exposes its chest, it's a threat. And to show that it submits, the mandrill shows its bum!

The German Shepherd Is a Gifted Dog!

Athletic and obedient, German shepherd dogs have many good qualities. They can be trained to be a guide dog, to detect drugs or weapons or to find people who have been buried after an avalanche or an earthquake.

The African Elephant's Mud Baths

Like rhinoceroses and hippopotamuses, elephants love to roll around in the mud. During the rainy season, they wade and lie down in the ponds that form in the savanna. By covering themselves from head to toe with clay, elephants protect themselves from insect bites and the heat of the sun.

The Rhinoceros Beetle: An Enormous Insect

This male rhinoceros beetle is impressive not only because of its size, approximately 6 inches (16 mm), but also for the horns, which are in the shape of claws, on its head. It uses its horns to grab objects, to fight and to attract females.

The Southern Right Whale's Baleen

This big marine mammal from the southern hemisphere mostly eats krill, a small crustacean. To capture them, the whale takes a big gulp of water that it then lets out through its baleen. The baleen allows the whale to filter out the water and keep only its prey in its mouth.

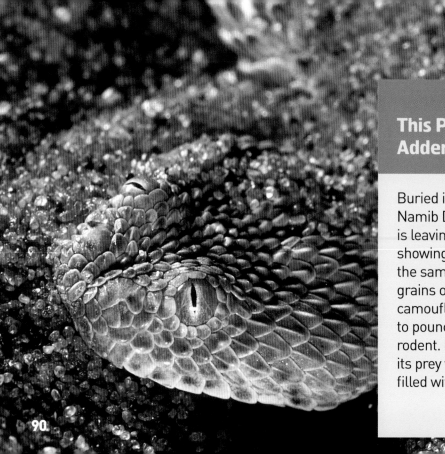

This Peringuey's Adder Is Alert

Buried in the sand of the Namib Desert, this viper is leaving only its head showing. Its scales are the same color as the grains of sand, and, fully camouflaged, it's ready to pounce on a lizard or rodent. It will then bite its prey with its fangs filled with deadly venom.

The Golden Marmoset Is a Protected Species

In order to protect the golden marmoset, its habitat is being protected. Certain forests where it lives are no longer being exploited. It can therefore continue to live there, along with the other animals that also make these forests their home. In the 1970s, there were only 200 of these monkeys remaining. However, there are now more than 1,000.

This Hornet Has Five Eyes

The hornet's two big eyes allow it to see. Made up of a mosaic of thousands of sensors, these "facetted eyes" don't provide a precise image but are particularly adapted to detect movement. The three small eyes, arranged in a triangle, are simply light detectors. They allow hornets to direct themselves in relation to the sun.

The Fragile Animals of the Seabed

Sponges and corrals are magnificent marine animals, but they are threatened by pollution, tourism and destructive fishing techniques. However, these colorful animals are indispensable to the ecology of the seabed: they are a refuge for a large number of fish, crustaceans and mollusks.

The Bobcat: A Solitary Hunter

Agile and supple, the bobcat, which lives in North America, has a great sense of balance. It hunts small prey such as mice or rabbits. It must also be vigilant: this hunter is also hunted. Pumas, wolves and coyotes kill them to avoid having to compete with them for territory and prey.

An Ostrich Chick Hatches from Its Egg

The ostrich that is helping this chick is probably not its mother, but rather the dominant female of the harem. This female, along with the male, incubated all the eggs. She started by choosing the nest among the many the male dug. The females of the harem, between two and six of them, then laid their eggs in it.

95

Sandfish: "Swimmer" of the Desert

It may be called sandfish, but it's definitely a lizard. The sandfish's airtight eyelids and soft scales allow it to easily and comfortably slide in the sand. As soon as a predator threatens this species of skink, it burrows! It can dig many feet down into the sand.

The Hooded Seal's Nose

What appears to be a ball balanced on this seal's head is actually the end of its nose! This "hood," which lengthens the nose of males, gave the species its name. It's a kind of pouch that the male, at the moment of reproduction, inflates to intimidate those who might want to seduce his females.

Some Very Helpful Gray Langurs

This dog is getting some help from two langurs, a species of Indian monkey, to rid it of its fleas. There is no power struggle here, as is often the case in such grooming sessions between a less dominant species and a more dominant one. These monkeys simply decided to be helpful!

Educating the Baird's Tapir

The male tapir only lives with the female during mating, which lasts barely two days. The female is then left to nurse her young for a year. If it survives, the baby will end up weighing over 600 pounds (300 kg) if it's a male. The Baird's tapir is the largest of the American tapirs.

Kangaroo Combat

Male kangaroos sometimes fight each other to choose a leader within the group or to attract a female. Upright on their hind legs, they try to unbalance their rival with their front paws. They scratch each other as well, but the wounds are never fatal.

Bees: Veritable Architects

Bees construct their honeycombs with the wax they produce. They deposit their eggs in them, as well as the honey that will be consumed by both the bee babies and the adults. In nature, bees make their hives in tree hallows or in rocks. Beekeepers, however, build them wooden hives that allow them to easily retrieve the honey.

The Shrike's Pantry

This shrike transports small prey in its beak and bigger prey, which sometimes weigh as much as it does, in its claws. The shrike hangs its prey on a thorn, a barbed wire or from a branch and then flies away. It will return to retrieve its meal when it's hungry.

A Prairie Rattlesnake Sounds the Alarm

This rattlesnake is rolled up in a coil and resting. But beware if you bother it! It can measure more than 5 feet (1.6 m) and its bite can be fatal. Luckily, if you get too close, the rattlesnake will warn you of the impending danger with the rattle, made of dried scales, at the end of its tail.

The Long-Tailed Weasel Is Not a Toy

The long-tailed weasel, although very cute, is like every other weasel — a formidable carnivore. Its small size, ranging from 6½ inches to just under 10 inches (20–25 cm), allows it to slide into even the narrowest rodent tunnels. Weasels kill rodents by piercing their prey's skull with their pointy teeth.

The Domestic Goose Is Not White

A large bird with brown or gray plumage, geese mainly eat grass. However, when they're raised to produce foie gras, they are force-fed, corn mostly, for many days to swell their liver. Geese are also raised for their down, which is used to make very warm jackets and duvets.

The Gluttony of the Minotaur Beetle

The minotaur beetle is a type of dung beetle, a small insect that feasts on cow dung or horse manure, which it forms into balls with the help of its wide, flat front legs. These beetles are very useful: they bury the balls to save them for later, which helps fertilize grass.

The Fox Squirrel: An Egg Thief

Fox squirrels spend part of their time on the ground looking for nuts, seeds and insects. They spend the rest of their time in trees, where they are sheltered from birds of prey and can eat their meal or perhaps find another meal — by stealing the eggs from a bird's nest. The fox squirrel got its name from the color of its fur, which is similar to that of a fox.

This Armadillo Can Roll Itself into a Ball

The three-banded armadillo rolls into itself into a ball for protection. It is the only armadillo that can do this. Armadillos use their long claws to defend themselves, but they mostly use their claws to search the ground for food, such as worms, small insects and tubers.

The Japanese Macaque: The Snow Monkey

Thanks to their thick fur, these monkeys can tolerate temperatures below 30°F (0°C). During periods of extreme cold, they bask in warm water sources created by volcanoes. When there are no longer any leaves, fruit or insects, the macaque eats tree bark.

Barn Owls: A White Owl in the Dark Night

This owl often makes its nest in towers or steeples, but it also likes to settle in attics, holes in trees and similar shelters. Also known as the "white owl," its snow-white chest is clearly visible under its wings when it flies.

Is the Wolf Spider a Monster?

Seen from above, this spider has a head that looks like a monster's. It is, however, not a cruel animal. It is actually a very ordinary spider and is happy to simply catch prey in its web. It can be found in wetlands, flooded prairies and around springs in Europe.

The Caimans Are Threatened

Caimans live in South America, close to their North American cousins, the alligators. They like warming themselves in the sun, which make them easy targets for poachers, who kill them for their skin, which is used to make bags and shoes.

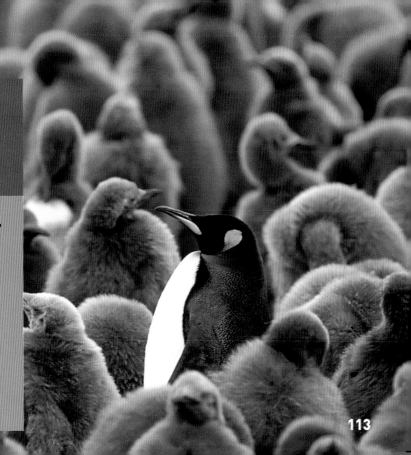

The King Penguin: From Brown Pajamas to Black-and-White Suit

While the adults are fishing, the young penguins gather in the nursery by the thousands. Later they'll lose their brown down, which will be replaced by black, white and orange feathers. This waterproof and dense plumage allows them to swim in the cold waters of Antarctica.

The Pygmy Hippopotamus: Not So Small...

This baby pygmy hippopotamus will become an adult measuring almost 6 feet (1.8 m) long and just under 2½ feet (75 cm) tall and weighing around 440 pounds (200 kg)! However, its size is certainly less impressive than its cousin the common hippopotamus, which weighs over 2¼ tons (2 metric tons) as an adult. The pygmy hippopotamus lives in West Africa.

The Long Arms of the White-Handed Gibbon

Due to their long arms, gibbons are the most agile and fastest of all monkeys. They use their arms to move from branch to branch and lift them to balance themselves when they walk. They are the only monkeys to be able to walk without putting their hands on the ground.

The Potato Beetle: Devourer of Potato Plant Leaves

During the summer, the female potato beetle lays 2,500 eggs, in clutches of 20 to 30. Well sheltered under the leaves of potato plants, they hatch after four to 10 days. The larvae have ferocious appetites and can ravage potato plants.

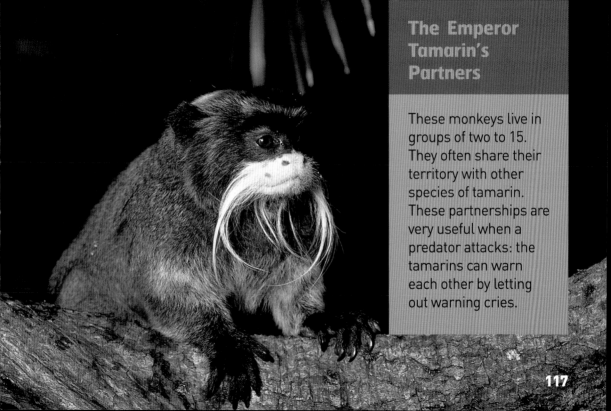

The Emperor Tamarin's Partners

These monkeys live in groups of two to 15. They often share their territory with other species of tamarin. These partnerships are very useful when a predator attacks: the tamarins can warn each other by letting out warning cries.

The Sweetlips: A Victim Like so Many Other Fish

Each year, millions of fish, such as this sweetlips, are captured in tropical waters and sold in the pet trade, to live in aquariums. These fish sell well as they aren't very expensive. However, a large number of them die when captured or while being transported.

The White-Nosed Coati: A Fake Vegetarian

This cousin of the raccoon eats fruit almost exclusively when they grow in abundance. The rest of the year, the coati is an omnivore: it eats everything. Its flexible nose and the powerful claws of its front paws allow it to unearth insects, lizards and even well-hidden small mammals.

The Polar Bear Cub's Games

Everything is an excuse to play for this bear cub: fighting, somersaults in the snow, sliding on the ice or even games with found objects. The cub's mother takes advantage of these moments to teach it skills that will be useful in its adult life, such as when hunting.

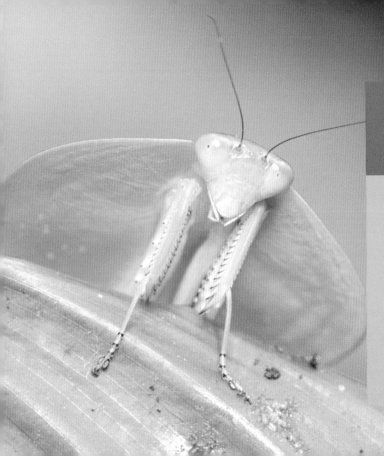

The Mantis: Tiger of the Grass

Motionless and almost invisible in the green grass, the praying mantis waits for its prey. When prey arrives, the mantis deploys its thorny legs as fast as lightning and captures it. Then the mantis breaks the prey's neck and devours it. It's no surprise this big insect is nicknamed the "tiger of the grass."

A Spotted Hyena Laughing in the Setting Sun

Hyenas hunt in a pack during the evening and at night. During the day, they rest in their den, which they dug out of the ground or set among big rocks. They are not discreet! Hyenas let out numerous cries, including their famous laugh, during mating season.

The Peaceful Crabeater Seal Rests on an Ice Floe

Lying on the ice, this crabeater seal isn't cold. It is protected by a thick layer of fat and by its circulatory system, which efficiently distributes heat throughout its body. In addition to isolating it from the cold, its anatomy makes this seal an excellent swimmer, thanks to its smooth coat and its flippers.

123

These Northern Flicker Chicks Are Cramped!

This small entrance seems very impractical, but it prevents predators from entering the nest and eating the chicks. As adults, northern flickers barely weigh 3½ ounces (100 g). They dig their nests in pieces of wood, hallowed out dead trees or fence posts and lay four to nine eggs.

The Hartebeest's Aerial Gallop

Both male and female hartebeests have long, narrow heads with two long horns. Like other African antelopes, this mammal is a very good runner, which gives it a good chance of escaping from lions and cheetahs.

The Brown Bear Awakens

Brown bears store fat in the fall, and in winter, when food is scarce, they find a den in which to hibernate for the season. During this time, the bear's body functions at a slower rate, drawing from its fat reserves. If the temperature warms up, the bear might wake up and look for food.

A Shell on a Starfish

This small snail shell measuring just over half an inch (1.5 cm) in diameter spends its life on a starfish. In fact, the snail pricks the starfish and feeds on the liquid, called hemolymph, that circulates inside the starfish, which is the equivalent of blood in humans. This weakens the starfish but doesn't kill it.

The Male Mandarin Is So Beautiful!

As is the case with many birds, male and female mandarins don't look alike. The female has brown and white feathers, while the male sports superb colors to seduce her. This duck, originally from China and Japan, lives in ponds surrounded by trees and shrubs.

The Okapi Is a Bit of a Contortionist

The okapi's tongue is so elastic and its neck so flexible that, when it washes itself, it can reach every part of its body, something no other mammal can do. It can even lick its own ears! No wonder its fur always looks impeccable.

The Graceful Flight of the Dragonfly

The dragonfly doesn't collect nectar from flowers; it is happy to simply land on them. It prefers to feed on small insects, which it captures mid-flight. With its two pairs of wings, it flies wonderfully. It can fly in place or move very quickly. Certain species can even fly backward!

This Japanese Crane Is in Full Display

These cranes can hold elegant poses, jump and bow, wings spread out, legs horizontal or vertical, in a magnificent ballet. These dances have a precise goal for young males: to seduce a female.

The Muskrat's Beautiful Teeth

This rodent has four superb incisors measuring almost an inch (2 cm) long. It uses them to eat aquatic plants but also to build dens, like a beaver. Behind the muskrat's incisors, a sort of second top lip closes its mouth, which allows it to gnaw underwater without taking in water.

The Two-Toed Sloth Is a Great Sleeper!

This sloth, which only has two toes on its front legs, can sleep up to 18 hours a day and moves very slowly. This makes it easy prey for hawks and felines. However, since it moves so little, it can hide perfectly among branches, which makes it difficult to spot.

Northern Gannets Are Faithful Couples

Every year, after spending many months apart at sea, the male and female gannet reunite at their nest. It is made of dirt, marine plants and feathers and is sometimes reinforced with their droppings. The female lays an egg, which she incubates, alternating with the male. When their chick can manage on its own, the parents once again take to the sea.

The Arctic Fox: White in Winter, Brown in Summer

When spring arrives, the arctic fox swaps its thick white fur for a lighter brown coat. They hunt in small groups during the winter, but they are more solitary in the summer, traveling long distances in search of prey.

A Baby Baboon and Its Mother

The female baboon gives birth to only one baby at a time. The young monkey stays with its mother for over a year, often gripped to her belly, trying to nurse. The mother teaches the baby the group's hierarchy and rules. Baboons live in rocky or wooded areas of Africa.

A Komodo Dragon Tastes the Air with Its Tongue

When looking for food, the Komodo dragon uses its tongue to pick up fragrant particles in the air. Measuring over 8 feet (2.5 m) and weighing over 250 pounds (165 kg), it is the biggest lizard in the world. It only lives on four small islands in Indonesia.

The Dromedary's Hump: A Mobile Pantry

When the dromedary eats a lot, a reserve of fat forms in its hump. If vegetation runs out, it relies on this reserve and can go many days without eating. The hump gets smaller as a result, but it starts to reflate as soon as the animal eats.

The Australian Short-Necked Turtle

This little turtle measuring up to 12 inches (30 cm) is found in rivers and ponds of Oceania, where it feeds on mollusks and small amphibians. Unlike most turtles, the male and female Australian short-necked turtle position themselves belly to belly to mate.

The Western Gray Kangaroo Can Finally Come Out

This young kangaroo has become too big and too heavy for its mother's pouch. However, she will continue to take care of her young. At the slightest sign of danger, the joey comes right back to huddle with its mother for protection. A baby kangaroo only becomes independent after its first birthday.

Traces of a Scarab Beetle Across the Desert

The desert is filled with signs of life. We can see traces of wind, water and of animals that walk, eat and rest there. Here, a scarab beetle's body has left a long, continuous trace; add that to the small crescent-shaped prints left by its legs, and you've got what looks like a spine.

The Hares' Violent Combat

During mating season, male hares engage in veritable battles to decide who will mate with the female. Throughout the night, they initiate fights that can last until the wee hours of the morning and that sometimes end with serious injuries.

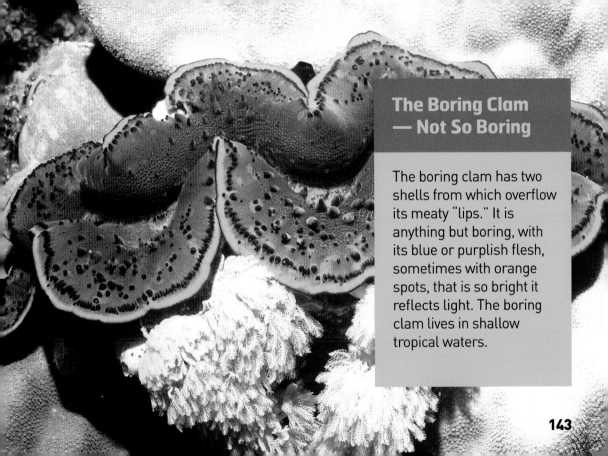

The Boring Clam — Not So Boring

The boring clam has two shells from which overflow its meaty "lips." It is anything but boring, with its blue or purplish flesh, sometimes with orange spots, that is so bright it reflects light. The boring clam lives in shallow tropical waters.

The Abert's Squirrel Dresses in Gray and White

North American squirrels have a gray coat, unlike European squirrels, which often have a red or brown coat. Although most mammals prefer going out at night to avoid predators, squirrels, being more agile and quick, are very active during the day.

The Jaguar: A Ruthless Killer

What an amazing yawn! This jaguar is showing off its fangs and terrifying jaws. A powerful predator of the tropical forests of America, the jaguar can kill prey four times its weight by breaking their neck. It can also knock them out by hitting them over the head with its paws.

The Mandarinfish Has Beautiful Skin Without Scales

Mandarinfish, also called dragonets, are very colorful fish. Striped of scales, they have a thin, oily film on their bodies that protects them from parasites and certain skin diseases.

The Fox: A Not-so-Courageous Hunter

Foxes feed mostly on small mammals such as field mice and voles. This fox probably found this pheasant when it was already dead. One of the fox's hunting techniques involves waiting, silent and lurking, until attainable prey passes by. It then pounces on it and chokes it to death. The fox then isolates itself to eat.

147

The Hippopotamus: Tranquil but Very Sensitive

These hippos seem very peaceful amid these aquatic plants, but if an intruder enters their territory, they will charge and threaten it with their 3¼ tons (3 metric tons) of weight and 15-inch (40 cm) canines. Hippopotamuses kill more humans annually than do lions.

Mouflon: Lord of the Mountains

The male mouflon is very recognizable in a group thanks to its superb spiral horns. In the fall, the sound of horns knocking into each other can be heard from miles away during the battles to attract the females. Generally, these fights don't leave anyone injured.

Meerkats Aren't Scared of Anything!

Meerkats know how to catch spiders and scorpions without getting bit. They also don't hesitate to attack snakes, even though this can be dangerous for them. These small mammals from Southern Africa live in packs and sometimes work together when attacking prey.

Very Vulnerable Baby Ostriches

This ostrich mother will have a lot of difficulty protecting her young if felines or scavengers attack. The only way out for them is to run, but the ostrich chicks don't run as fast as their parents. Out of the 20 to 30 chicks born, only a few will become beautiful adult ostriches.

The Stick Insect's Disguises

In the grass, we think it's a stem. In the woods, it looks like a twig. The stick insect lands on vegetation that has the same shape and coloring as it. Disguised in this way, this animal, which lives in the tropics and in the Mediterranean, avoids being an easy prey for birds and other insect eaters.

The Sperm Whale: A Champion Under Water

The presence of octopus and squid in the stomach of this sperm whale proves that it can dive over a mile under water! This mammal can remain under water for two hours without going up to the surface to breathe. And it has the largest brain of the entire animal kingdom!

The Cicada's Transformation

It all begins with eggs laid by a female in the branches of a shrub. Then the larvae come out of the eggs and fall to the ground. The larvae then dig tunnels and eat sap from tree roots. After many years, the larvae become cicadas and fly away, but they will only survive for a few weeks.

Verreaux's Sifaka: A Well-Attached Baby!

For this sifaka mother, one of numerous species of Madagascar lemurs, traveling in the open between two wooded areas is always dangerous — a predator could appear anytime. She always crosses such unsheltered areas very quickly, her baby gripped on her back. They will be safe once they are perched in the trees.

The Hermann's Tortoise Doesn't Need Dentures

The mouth of the Hermann's tortoise, like that of all tortoises, has no teeth. Its jaw is covered by a sharp horn, which allows it to chop plants, grasses or fruit and to tear up insects and snails. This tortoise, measuring 6 to 8 inches (16–20 cm) in length, has a tail that ends in a spike!

This Colt Is Taking Another Few Sips

Fifteen minutes after its birth, this donkey colt was already standing so it could suckle its mother. Here, at the age of two weeks, the colt drinks 3 to 6 quarts (3–6 L) of milk per day and is already chewing on grass. It will take six months to transition fully from milk to water, when it will eat over 17 pounds (8 kg) of grass and thistles per day.

The Stunning Puss Moth Caterpillar

Tail raised and head turned, this caterpillar is trying to scare away a predator. What a look! The caterpillars from this family have strange characteristics, evocative of their names, including "lobster moth" and "iron prominent."

The White Stork: An Incredible Builder

In the spring, after a long migration, the white stork returns home to Europe to mate. This wader builds its nest with twigs and grass. Some nests are improved upon year after year and end up becoming gigantic.

Bonobos Are Very Social Apes

Bonobos are difficult to observe in nature. Not well-known, these primates have a reputation for being pacifists. They live in groups and will initiate sexual intercourse to calm each other during conflicts.

Belugas Emit Ultrasounds

This marine mammal lives near Arctic ice floes. Like all cetaceans, it hunts and guides itself by emitting ultrasounds that bounce off its environment and its prey. This tracking system is inside the beluga's skull, which explains in part the bump on its forehead.

The Impala:
Champion Jumper

The impala can execute jumps over 32 feet (10 m) long and almost 10 feet (3 m) high. As soon as it spots a predator, this antelope warns the other herbivores with a type of dance. Then it launches into a crazy race, consisting of jumps and speeds reaching up to 37 miles per hour (60 km/h).

The Ant Queen's Many Eggs

A single queen ant can lay hundreds of thousands of eggs each month! As soon as they are laid, they are taken away by worker ants and placed one next to the other. Larvae will hatch from these eggs, and the larvae will eventually become nymphs and then ants.

A Caracara on a Capybara

With its sharp eyes, the caracara can warn the capybara, the biggest rodent in the world, of any danger — it flies away screaming. In exchange, the bird benefits from the insects that capybaras unearth. These rodents live in big families that can make insects and other small creatures flee when they move.

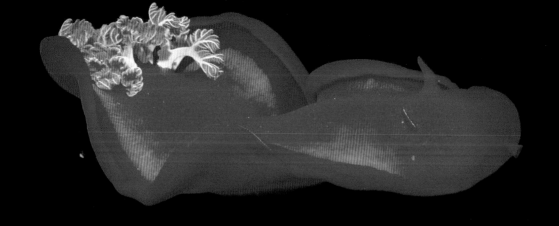

The Spanish Dancer's Beautiful Dress

The Spanish dancer is a mollusk without a shell. It undulates the flounces of its red dress to propel itself in the water. But this beauty remains on alert! Its antennae can detect intruders simply by their odor or by their movements in the water.

165

Whooper Swans Have a Voice

Whooper swans gather every winter on frozen Lake Kussharo, in Japan, to have singing competitions to seduce a female. Neck extended and wings spread out, the swan that sings best will be awarded the victory. Once the female is won over, the couple will mate for life.

166

This Boxer Crab Is Hiding His Claws in Sea Anemones Gloves

The boxer crab and the sea anemone get along famously. The crab wears the anemones on its claws and uses the venomous animal as a shield in case of danger. In exchange, the anemones get a free ride and can thereby find food more easily.

The Ocelot's Hunting Techniques

To surprise their prey — rodent, bird, monkey, armadillo, anteater — ocelots stick their belly against the ground and crawl toward them. When they're at the perfect distance, these small felines rise up, chase their prey, leap on it and kill it by biting its neck.

The Brazilian Tapir Loves Water

This South American mammal spends a lot of its time in water. It goes in to cool off and to eat aquatic plants, but it also uses water to elude predators like jaguars and pumas. The tapir's paws have three wide digits that prevent it from sinking in the mud.

The Tropical Striped Triplefin:
A Fan of Coral

This small fish, measuring just over 2 inches (5 cm) long, lives in coral reefs 10 to 30 feet (3–10 m) under water. We often see it stopped on coral or sponges. Like gobies, to which they are closely related, the tropical striped triplefin roams the seafloor in search of worms and mollusks.

Wombats Start off Very Small But Get Very Big

At birth, wombat joeys measure just over an inch (3 cm) and only weighs $\frac{1}{30}$ ounce (1 g)! The mother carries her baby in a ventral pouch while it is growing. Six to nine months later, the baby wombat can leave the pouch but will remain in its underground nest until its first birthday.

What Big Teeth the Walrus Has!

The walrus's ivory tusks can reach nearly 20 inches (50 cm) long for the female and over 3 feet (1 m) for the male — and they never stop growing! These gigantic canines are useful for the walrus to, among other things, move itself around. Thus, to get out of the water and to scale ice, the walrus sticks its tusks in like an ice ax.

The Southern Masked Weaver: Artisan of the Savanna

The female weaver doesn't joke around when it comes to the quality of the nest the male has built for her! Before moving in, she inspects it from every angle. The weaving, achieved using fresh and pliable grass, must not let through the African rain. The room must also be comfortable and big enough to accommodate the two or three eggs she'll lay.

The Scorpion: A Real Carnivore

Scorpions eat snakes and insects. After immobilizing their prey with their pincers, they tear it to pieces with their mandible, which is shaped like pincers and located above their mouth. They then eat their prey alive. Scorpions only use their venom, which is inside the end of their tail, to defend themselves.

174

The Octopus's Eight Arms

Equipped with hundreds of suckers, the arms of the octopus, also called tentacles, have multiple functions. Octopuses use their tentacles to crawl, swim, catch prey, defend themselves, build their shelter and reproduce. And if something happens and a tentacle is cut, no worries, they heal — and grow back!

The Jerboa: Racer of the Desert

Supported by its long back legs, jerboas travel the desert in giant leaps, like a kangaroo. They're the fastest of the small rodents and can go faster than 12 miles per hour (20 km/h)! But this mode of travel is very tiring, forcing jerboas to hunt at night, when it's cooler.

Crickets Walk, Jump, Fly...

Crickets can walk and jump using their powerful back legs. They can also fly, by spreading their wings. But their legs and wings also help them be heard: when a cricket rubs them together, it produces a piercing sound that changes according to the speed of the rubbing.

The Eared Seal: Land or Sea Animal

The morphology of the eared seal, and specifically the envelopes surrounding its fingers, which form a sort of flipper, allow it to swim easily. But eared seals are also capable of moving around on land, by leaning on their long posterior and anterior limbs.

The Wild Boar's Protective Coat

The boar piglets' brown and cream coat camouflages them well among the leaves and mosses of the forest. They can sleep peacefully! From the age of five or six months, when they are less vulnerable, they trade in their camouflage coat for a brown one.

The Stag: King of the Forest

Every February, stags lose their antlers, but new ones start growing in the spring. Their antlers are covered with brown velvet that the stag sloughs off by rubbing them against trees. In September, during mating season, he fights other males with his antlers to attract the females.

The Dragonfly's Last Molt

Before becoming a beautiful winged insect, the dragonfly is a larva that lives in ponds and marshes. During its development, it molts many times: it leaves its skin and creates a new one to fit its size. The dragonfly only forms its two back pairs of wings during its last molt. It then leaves its larva suit and flies away.

A Mother Fox and Her Kits in Their Den

In the spring, the fox gives birth to a litter of three to six kits. The first month, settled in a den filled with grass, leaves and hair, the mother nurses her babies. Then they feed on prey caught by their father and predigested by their mother.

The Steller's Sea Eagle: The Biggest Fishing Eagle

Everything about this eagle is spectacular. It's long beak, crooked and sharp, allows it to kill big prey and rip their flesh. With its wingspan of over 8 feet (2.5 m) and its tail that opens like a Japanese fan, it truly is a master glider.

This Doe Is on Alert

Well hidden in ferns, this doe opens her eyes wide and sticks up ears, ready to shelter herself in the thick forest if she feels threatened. The male deer, called bucks, are as suspicious and cautious as the does. They often wait until nightfall to leave the woods.

184

The Perilous Migration of the Wildebeest

In Africa, no less than 1.5 million wildebeests travel hundreds of miles each year in search of green pastures. Many of these antelopes drown or are devoured by crocodiles during river crossings.

The Octopus's Discreet Propulsion

Octopuses slither along the seabed using their eight tentacles. In the open sea, they propel themselves by letting out water that they have previously absorbed. They also have a pouch full of ink, a black liquid they can launch onto a predator to mask their getaway.

The Cautious European Rabbit

European rabbits never stray farther than a few hundred feet from their den, fearful of predators. During the day, they often remain hidden in a tuft of grass or in a cultivated field. Ever cautious, they mostly feed in the evening or at night.

Stalked Barnacles: A Threatened Shellfish

Stalked barnacles, also called goose barnacles, are a crustacean that lives on rocks along ocean shores. A culinary delicacy that is in high demand, it has been overfished and is disappearing from certain areas. Like many other fish and shellfish, its survival is threatened despite fishing regulations.

The Argiope Spider Gets Its Meals Delivered

A fly just got caught in this spider's web. The spider will immediately sting it to anesthetize it and then wrap it in its silk cocoon. Before eating this "mummy," the spider sprays it with digestive sugars to soften it. All that's left is for the spider to sip up this delicious mash.

The Green Iguana Doesn't Need Air Conditioning

Like all cold-blooded animals, the green iguana is very sensitive to excess heat and cold. To adapt to the ambient temperature, it is endowed with a piece of skin under its throat, called the dewlap. If it's hot, the iguana unfolds it to increase the surface of its skin to help dissipate the heat.

The Lilian's Lovebird Is Beautiful — When Left in Nature!

The Lilian's lovebird, which lives in the forests and wooded savannas of Africa, is so cute that it is captured to be sold, most often abroad, in the pet trade. But it is worth knowing that for every 10 of these birds that are captured, only one on average survives being captured, transported and being confined in a cage.

The Alpine Ibex Doesn't Have Vertigo!

The alpine ibex is a remarkable climber that roams steep rock walls with ease. During the summer, this wild goat climbs to the least visited areas of the Alps, where it lives. There it finds grass and small branches, which make up its favorite meal.

A Small Elephant Will Become Big

As a newborn, this baby elephant already weighs more than 220 pounds (100 kg) and drinks almost 3 gallons (11 l) of milk a day! Its mother still protects it, since its baby tusks aren't any bigger than human canine teeth! Its tusks won't be visible until it's two years old.

Red Rock Crabs Are Beautiful and Useful

These active, brightly colored crabs clean the rocks and beaches where they live by eating algae, dead fish and miscellaneous debris. Red rock crabs live in communities in the Galapagos Islands, the archipelago on the coast of the equator that is famous for its unique wildlife.

The Snow Leopard: Feline of the Mountains

These young snow leopards will soon leave their parents to conquer their own territory: vast expanses located at an altitude between 8,000 to 16,000 feet (2,500–5,000 m). Their thick fur allows them to withstand the cold and snow of the long winters in the forests and steppes of the Himalayas.

Pigs Are Real Gluttons!

The pig is a domestic animal. It uses its snout to search the ground for food. Its feet have four wide and robust digits that allow it to scratch the ground without sinking too deep into the mud. Pigs are voracious and hardly ever refuse food.

The Dragonfly Has Good Eyesight

The dragonfly's two big eyes cover almost its entire head. Each one is made up of almost 30,000 small eyes that provide a very precise and wide view — the dragonfly can almost see what is happening behind it! Flies with their head in the clouds will quickly be swallowed in flight.

The Varied Meals of the Black-Headed Gull

This young gull eats the food that its parents regurgitate for it. On the menu is worm mush, insects, vegetation and garbage. In fact, these black-headed gulls feed on just about everything they find. This small gull has a cry that sounds like a laugh.

198

Hyacinth Macaws Are "Married" for Life

Very loyal, hyacinth macaws pair up for life. To make their nest, they choose a tree with soft wood. Thanks to their strong beaks, they can dig a cavity in the tree trunk. Lastly, they cover the bottom of the nest with a layer of wood chips before depositing their eggs.

The Peaceful Red Panda

Red pandas, also named lesser pandas, spend a large part of their day sleeping in trees or on rocks. They also love to sunbathe. This very inactive mammal has a diet that reflects its low energy level: the red panda eats bamboo leaves almost exclusively.

The Red Deer's Call Is a Warning

The red deer vocalizes loud enough to be heard more than a mile away, which warns the other males that the females surrounding him are his. Red deers fiercely defend their harem against both young and old males that live outside of their herd.

It's All Fun and Games for These Little Lambs

These lambs have an easy life, jumping and playing all day! Born in the spring in litters of one to three, they are nursed by their mother for three to five months. Then, in the summer, they graze on grass in the fields. During the winter, they eat 2 to 4 pounds (1–2 kg) of hay and grains daily, provided by their human caretakers.

Would You Be Afraid of the Frilled-Neck Lizard?

If it's startled, the frilled-neck lizard, measuring around 8 inches (20 cm), spreads out its frill, which is usually flattened along the length of its body, opens its mouth wide and lets out a menacing scream. But if you don't back down, this fearful monster will likely just run away from you!

The Rearing of European Fire Ants

While other species of ants cultivate mushrooms, European fire ants raise aphids since the ants feed on a sweet liquid they expel. They keep the aphids in a sort of stable attached to their anthill, protecting them and taking great care of their eggs.

The European Plaice Is Always Ready to Bite

Plaice have a powerful jaw and particularly well-developed teeth. These allow them to crush the shells they find on the seabed, which they eat in addition to little fish. European plaice live on sandy surfaces at the bottom of the Mediterranean Sea and the North Atlantic.

205

The Black and White Panda Only Eats Greens

Living exclusively in China, pandas are big eaters of bamboo leaves. They dedicate 10 to 12 hours a day to feeding themselves, consuming 22 to 33 pounds (10–15 kg) of leaves. It's a very simple diet that allows newborns, which weigh only 3½ ounces (100 g), to become beautiful mammals weighing as much as 400 pounds (180 kg).

The Australian Pelican's Large Bill

This pelican, found in Australia, Papua New Guinea and Indonesia, opens its bill wide to defend itself, as if it were yawning, and to collect water when it's raining. They often use the pouch under their bill when fishing, to place a fish head first in their mouth before swallowing it.

Siamese Cats Have a Royal Background

The Siamese, a black and beige cat with blue eyes, is of royal origin. The breed once belonged exclusively to the king of Siam, present-day Thailand, and roamed freely in the palaces and temples. This feline didn't appear in Europe until the end of the 19th century, when it was brought back by an English consul and a French minister.

Common Genets Love Heights

Genets, cousins of the weasel, take refuge in the trees. They're good climbers and settle on wide branches or in holes to rest or to eat their prey. The genet can be found in Africa, Asia, Spain and France.

The Young Friesian's Coat

Friesians are usually brown at birth, but their coats become dark ebony as they reach adulthood. Very easily trained, these horses are often used in circuses and other shows. It is named after Friesland, the region of the Netherlands from which it originates.

The Pufferfish Plays Ball

When threatened, pufferfish fill their body with water and take the shape of a ball. By doing this, they can startle their enemies by making them believe they are much bigger than they actually are. The tactic is risky, however, since once a pufferfish is "inflated," it can barely move. Luckily, its spikes dissuade most predators from attacking.

A Young European Green Woodpecker's Meal

Using their thin beak, European green woodpeckers dig their nest in trees with soft, dead or decomposing wood. They also use their beak to extract larvae from trees riddled with woodworms. These woodpeckers also catch other insects using their big tongue, which is coated with saliva.

Harvester Ants Transport Seeds

Although most of the 9,000 species of ants on our planet eat a bit of everything, North American harvester ants prefer seeds. The worker ants chew the seeds and transform them into small balls that are consumed by the entire colony.

213

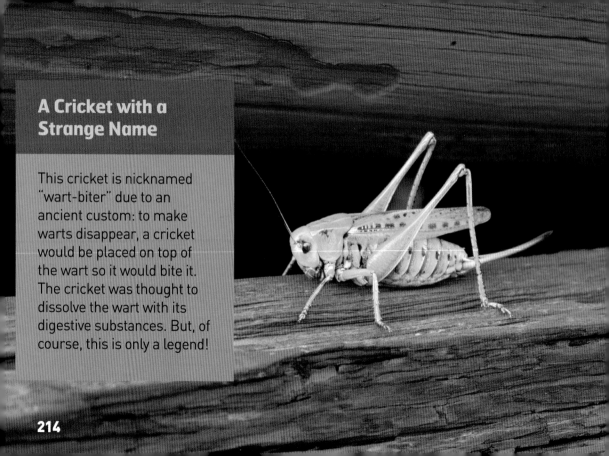

A Cricket with a Strange Name

This cricket is nicknamed "wart-biter" due to an ancient custom: to make warts disappear, a cricket would be placed on top of the wart so it would bite it. The cricket was thought to dissolve the wart with its digestive substances. But, of course, this is only a legend!

214

The Real Color of the Black Panther

All leopards are spotted, including the "black" leopard, which we call the black panther! Due to a genetic oddity, this leopard secretes more melanin, the substance that colors skin and hair, than the more commonly known "spotted" leopard. This makes its fur darker, but not uniform: you can still see some spots on its dark coat.

215

The Spider Crab's Long Legs

Spider crabs got their name because they look like spiders, with their narrow body and long legs. They are active during the daytime, eating mostly sea anemones. They sleep at night, thereby avoiding competition with common crabs, which feed by the light of the moon.

The Hippopotamuses' Violent Battles

Hippopotamuses live in groups and are lead by a male. When another male tries to take the place of the leader, battles break out. Each tries to intimidate the other. If neither submits, the two males can injure each other with very serious bites to the neck. 217

Orangutans Are Disappearing

Orangutans live in the tropical forests of the islands of Borneo and Sumatra, which are located in Indonesia and Malaysia. They are currently threatened. Their forest habitat is being destroyed through commercial exploitation and agriculture. In addition, poachers capture young apes to sell them alive, killing their mother in most cases.

Brown Owls Attack in the Silence of the Night

When it has located its prey, a brown owl charges without a sound: the soft down that borders its supple feathers stifles the sound of its flight. The owl then seizes its victim in its claws and brings it to a location where it will swallow it whole, without even taking the time to dismember it.

The Hedgehog Is a Big Sleeper

During the day, hedgehogs normally sleep hidden in shrubs or on a bunch of leaves. To take this photo, we had to turn it over. It's only at dusk and at night that hedgehogs become active. They spend a big part of their life sleeping, during the day but also for the entire winter! In fact, as soon as the end of fall hits, hedgehogs start hibernating and don't wake up until spring.

The Fennec: A Big-Eared Fox

Thanks to its ears, the fennec can locate mice and lizards, its favorite prey. The fennec also eats birds, insects and fruit. Although it can't go without eating, it can go weeks without drinking. Thus, it's perfectly adapted to the area in which it lives, the deserts of Africa and Asia.

This Bug Is a Coleopteran

This insect is a coleopteran, part of the Coleoptera order of beetles. The members of this order have six legs and a mouth adapted to chewing plants. They are also endowed with wings in the shape of sheaths (*koleos* in Greek, from where they get their name), which cover suppler wings when the insect is at rest. They use these wings to fly.

The Bottlenose Dolphin Is Fast Like the Wind

Their perfectly aerodynamic body, powerful tail and smooth skin coated with oil allow dolphins to go very fast on the water's surface as well as under water — they can reach speeds of over 40 miles per hour (70 km/h). However, it's when they jump that dolphins are fastest, since air offers less resistance than water.

223

To Each Zebra Its Stripes!

Zebras all look similar, but their stripes are very different: each zebra has its own pattern. It's thanks to these stripes that we can identify zebras within a herd, and we can differentiate the three species of African zebras from each other.

A Wild Boar Mother and Her Piglet

Like many animals, the young wild boar — called a piglet or "squeaker" — doesn't have the same coat as its parents. In a few months, this newborn will trade in its beige stripes for a brown coat. Its weight, of around 2 pounds (1 kg) at birth, can reach up to nearly 800 pounds (350 kg) for the biggest males.

The Ladybug's Dots

The most common ladybug has seven dots, but we also see in our gardens, in forests and even in our attics, where they hibernate, ladybugs with two, 10 or even 24 dots. The color of the elytrons, the wing-like shell that protects its real wings, varies from yellow to red.

This Atlantic Puffin Has Made a Nice Catch

Puffins mostly eat fish, which they catch by diving. When swimming back up to the surface, they trap their catch in their beak, with help from the spikes on their tongue and on the roof of their mouth. They then dive back in for their next catch. Once they've caught a good meal, they bring the fish back to their hiding place at the bottom of their burrow.

These Asian Elephants Are on a Family Outing

Asian elephants, just like their African cousins with big ears, live in family groups, often headed by an older female. She shares her experience with the rest of the group and makes the day-to-day decisions about the necessary movements to drink and eat.

The Male Wolf Imposes His Authority

According to the place he occupies within the pack, a male wolf will affirm his dominance or shows his submissiveness. He does this with the expression of his eyes, the orientation of his ears, the position of his tail and many other traits. When a wolf swells his mane, puts his ears up and shows his fangs like this wolf is doing, he is obviously showing dominance!

The Little Caiman Will Become Big

The sex of a baby caiman depends on the temperature inside the nest, which the female builds with plant debris in a mound of dirt. If the weather is nice, the eggs will be warm underground, and a majority of males will be born. If the temperature dips down, it is mostly females that will hatch.

The Greedy Lynx

At night, after a day of rest, lynxes are ready for hunting. They love deer and chamois, but they can content themselves with a squirrel or a marmot. More rarely, sheep end up on the menu. This is why farmers are always wary of the presence of a lynx.

The Tarantula Mother's Cocoon

In order to protect her hundreds of eggs, a female tarantula weaves a deep cocoon where she can delicately deposit them. She uses a very resistant floss to build this cradle, which she creates with the silk glands located under her belly. It's this same "silk factory" that allows her to weave her web.

232

The Small Wings of the Gentoo Penguin

The wings of the gentoo penguin are so small that it cannot fly. However, this bird swims better than some fish: it can propel itself almost 19 miles per hour (30 km/h) to catch them. Gentoo penguins return to land to build their nests and to spend the night. The rest of the time, they are in the water.

The Social Life of Prairie Dogs

North American prairie dogs live in families: one male, many females and their young. Families gather in large colonies, called "towns," which allow the members of these different families to help and protect each other. At the slightest hint of danger, a prairie dog will alert the others with a warning cry. A prairie dog town can include a few hundred to many thousands of individuals.

Greater Kudus Are Always on Guard

Greater kudus measure over 5 feet (1.6 m) at the withers and weigh more than 400 pounds (200 kg), but they are very nervous animals. When they drink, they are always ready to flee at the slightest suspicious sound, since Africa's big cats often roam watering holes in search of prey.

The North American Porcupine: A Very Prickly Rodent

The porcupine owes the second part of its name to the thousands of quills that cover its entire body, excluding its snout and belly. As to the first part, it's a mistake: it may look a bit like a pig, but there's nothing porky about a porcupine! It's actually a rodent. Very agile, porcupines can climb trees to eat leaves, flowers, berries, nuts and bark.

The Northern Goshawk: An Efficient Hunter

This powerful hawk hunts birds (such as jays, pigeons and ravens) and medium-sized mammals (such as squirrels, rabbits and voles). To feed their young, they sometimes steal chicks from other nests. They sometimes even eat other birds of prey!

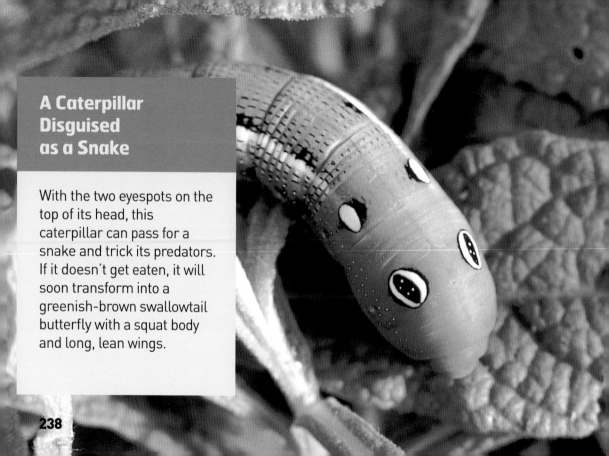

A Caterpillar Disguised as a Snake

With the two eyespots on the top of its head, this caterpillar can pass for a snake and trick its predators. If it doesn't get eaten, it will soon transform into a greenish-brown swallowtail butterfly with a squat body and long, lean wings.

Roosters Are not Wimps!

The rooster is without a doubt the king of the hen-house, but he is a benevolent king. His principal concern is protecting his hens and chicks. While they are feeding, the rooster keeps an eye on the surroundings, letting out a warning call at the slightest hint of danger. And if an intruder approaches, the rooster is ready to fight to the death.

The Seals' Vicious Combat

Male seals are the first to arrive at the mating site. They fight violently to win the territory before the arrival of the females, which will make up the victor's harem. If the male seals are evenly matched, their confrontations can last a long time and they can seriously injure each other, despite the very dense coats that protect them.

The Stag Beetle's Short Life

The stag beetle's larva lives for three years in deadwood before becoming this beautiful insect that will only live for a few weeks, which is just long enough for it to find a partner and reproduce. We call it a "stag" beetle since its jaw look like a stag's antlers.

Watch Out for the Sea Hawk!

The fishing sea hawk spots its prey by flying 30 to 60 feet (10–20 m m) above the water. It then dives and seizes it in its powerful talons. The sea hawk then brings its prey to a tree to eat it. Its coarse talons allow it to catch the most slippery fish.

The Formidable Jaws of the Bush Viper

The viper's two sharp, hinged fangs are folded when its mouth is closed. But if prey appears, they immediately jut out, and the viper bites the prey and injects it with deadly venom. Vipers can therefore swallow big rodents, such as this rat, in one bite.

The Skin of the Jackson's Chameleon

Like all chameleons, the Jackson's chameleon has the ability to change color, by modifying the concentration of the four colors contained in its skin. It can also create different nuances on its body that allow it to camouflage itself, to intimidate its enemies or even to contend with the heat — by adopting a lighter color.

The Ring-Tailed Lemur Marks Its Territory

To mark its territory, the ring-tailed lemur impregnates its wrists and tail with a repulsive liquid that it produces in glands under its arms. Thus, if it meets a rival, the lemur only needs to shake its long tail in the direction of its adversary in order to spread an odor that will chase that rival away.

The Northern Gannet Flies with the Wind

The northern gannet measures over 3¼ feet (1 m) long and has a wingspan that can reach close to 6 feet (1.8 m). It is so big that it can have trouble flying! To help them fly, northern gannets build their nests on cliffs or on top of island plateaus. From that height, they can take advantage of wind currents to help them take off.

The Giraffes' Neck Fights

These two young male giraffes are fighting to decide which one will rule the group of females and father their calves. They intertwine their necks and bang their shoulders and heads together. However, these impressive battles are never fatal, since the bones in the giraffe's skull are very solid.

A Young Fawn's Spotted Coat

At birth fawns have a dark coat covered with white spots. As the mother licks it, the lighter hairs fall out and darker ones appear. At the end of two to three months, the white dots disappear and the fawn's coat becomes brown.

West Indian Manatees: Protected but Still Threatened

West Indian manatees used to be hunted by humans for their flesh, skin and fat. It is prohibited to hunt them today, but manatees are still threatened: they can get stuck in fishing nets and killed by motorboats. They also suffer from the effects of pollution.

249

The Sooty Albatross's Destiny

Its parents feed the little sooty albatross for about four months before it leaves the nest. The chick won't return to the Indian Ocean island where it was born until it is three years old, at which time it will find a mating partner with whom to spend the rest of its life. Every two or three years, the female will lay a single egg.

In the Baboon's Footsteps

A big track for the foot, a smaller one for the hand. From their shape, scientists can identify the tracks of a baboon, a monkey from western and northern Africa. Like other monkeys, baboons move around by crawling. When they stop, they straighten up and "sit" on their back legs, freeing up their hands to catch food.

The Scallop: A Blue-Eyed Mollusk

Scallops have a soft body bordered by dozens of blue eyes that only see light, no details. If their enemy, the starfish, approaches, the tentacles between their eyes detect the vibrations of the water and the scallop will close its shell.

A Pale Little Tiger

This tiger's body doesn't produce enough color pigments, which explains its whiteness. In the wild, white tigers are rare. Around 1950, a maharajah captured two and bred them. This breed has since been conserved and developed in zoos around the world.

Unruly Little Egrets

Spats are frequent among little egrets, often involving pursuits, blows and screams. They squabble frequently and over just about everything — even in mid-flight! Although they are protected today, they were long hunted for their feathers, which were used to adorn hats.

The Little Shrew Is Voracious!

This pretty shrew is a formidable carnivore. It devours insects, worms and caterpillars. Very agile, shrews hunt just as well on land as on water, where they capture little fish, tritons and crustaceans. They also eat the equivalent of their own weight, around $1/3$ ounce (10 g), daily.

The King of the Savanna

Lions spend a large amount of their time resting and scanning the horizon. The males hunt very little, but they are the first to eat the prey caught by the lionesses. The male's role as leader is to protect his group's territory against the intrusion of other felines and to chase away predators and competitors.

The Highly Threatened Sea Turtle

After ripping through the shell of its egg, the turtle hatchling must crawl to the ocean without being caught by a bird. In the water, the sea turtle is easy prey for carnivorous fish. As an adult, it will again be threatened by fishing nets that could strangle it.

Leaf Beetles Have Big Appetites

The leaf beetle is a parasite of willow and poplar trees. These leaf eaters can wreak havoc when they reproduce too quickly. But its voracious appetite can also be useful: they are raised to combat weeds. As a result, we don't have to use pesticides that pollute our environment.

The Eurasian Lynx Is Very Shy

Along with the brown bear and the wolf, the Eurasian lynx is one of the big European predators. Like the other apex predators, it's only significant threat is humans. However, it's a cautious animal and completely harmless toward humans. This feline is primarily active at night. Lynxes are very difficult to encounter since they run away as soon as anyone approaches them.

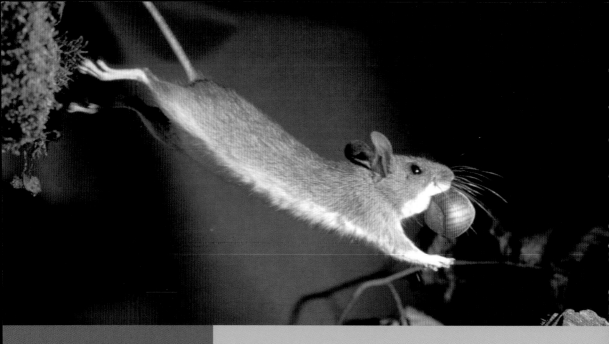

This Wood Mouse Is Doing a Swan Dive!

The wood mouse, measuring less than 4 inches (10 cm), can leap more than 30 inches (80 cm). If it finds a seed, nut, insect or worm, it rushes off to shelter itself from hawks and owls. It nests in hedges and shrubs, on the edge of fields or in forests.

Warthogs Have Big Teeth

This mammal lives in the tropical regions of Africa. Its curved top canines stick out of its mouth. Since they don't wear down by rubbing against other teeth, they become long and serve as tusks. To feed itself, the warthog grazes in an unusual way: on the knees of its front legs.

The Hawk: A Ruthless Bird of Prey

On the lookout from a branch or a post, hawks can spend hours looking for prey, usually a vole or a field mouse. Once the hawk has spotted one, it launches itself, stretching out its legs forward, and it kills it with its claws. Then it tears it to pieces with its crooked beak and eats it or brings it to its young.

The Tarantula's Particularity

Tarantulas only have four pairs of legs. The fifth pair in the front isn't a pair of legs at all. They are small members, which the tarantula uses to catch insects and to dig and feel the earth. Those of the male also have a small organ at the end, which it uses to introduce its semen into the body of the female when they are mating.

Impalas and Red-Billed Oxpeckers Are Good Friends

The red-billed oxpecker does the impala, a species of antelope, a big favor by eating the parasitic insects that live in its coat and can weaken it or even transmit diseases to it. But the impala isn't the only lucky one: this bird also rids other big African herbivores, such as buffalo, giraffes and rhinoceros, of their ticks and leeches.

The Dangerous Bluespotted Ribbontail Stingray

Bluespotted ribbontail stingrays live in sandy, coral-filled areas of the Indian Ocean, the Red Sea and Southeast Asia. They hunt shrimp, worms and crabs. When resting, they bury themselves in the sand, leaving only their eyes uncovered. Swimmers, watch your feet! This stingray has two venomous stingers on the base of its tail.

The Bison Is a Survivor

Around 1830, white men in North America started slaughtering almost all the bison in order to eat them or to deprive the Aboriginal peoples of this animal, which was indispensable to their survival. By 1890, the bison population had been reduced from 50 million to less than 1,000. Protected since 1905, they are once again plentiful in American national parks and nature reserves.

Upside Down, Right Side Up — Behold the Snail!

How come this snail isn't falling off this leaf? In its mouth, it produces sticky mucus that it deposits under itself as it moves. Since the visible part of its body, called the "foot," is in the shape of a suction cup, the snail can stick to stems and leaves and can even move upside down!

Why Are Flamingoes Pink?

White and gray at birth, flamingoes owe their bright color to the pink shrimp they eat. The color reaches its peak intensity when the flamingo is four to five years old. Flamingoes capture shrimp and other small animals and plants by filtering water through the lamellas that line their beak.

The Black-backed Jackal's Coat

This African black-backed jackal owes its name to the gray-black patch on the back of its coat. Jackals are good hunters that feed on birds, lizards, small mammals and carrion.

Giraffes Have Long Tongues!

With its long neck, measuring almost 10 feet (3 m), giraffes can reach the highest leaves of the acacias trees. They reach them with the help of their long, muscular tongue, which measures over 15 inches (40 cm). The giraffe isn't afraid of eating the thorns either; its mouth has a very resistant lining.

The Spike-Topped Apple Snail Is an Unusual Snail

The spike-topped apple snail has two distinct respiratory systems: gills that allow it to take in air under water, like a fish, and lungs, which allow it to breathe above water. This snail can be found in ponds, marshes and rivers in South and Central America.

Armadillos Can Go Just About Anywhere in Africa

The armadillo's body is covered with an armor of osteoderms, which protect it while ensuring it is still flexible. Thanks to its osteoderms, this mammal can easily slide into the tunnels it has dug using its powerful claws. Despite their short legs, armadillos are capable runners and, when threatened, take shelter at the bottom of their burrow.

The Greater Flamingo Is a Fine Ballerina

The greater flamingo leaps to take off and fly away. It runs in shallow water then rises up above the water. Disturbed by humans, these birds stopped living in the Camargue in the 1960s. Since then, thanks to an island reserved especially for them, they have returned in huge numbers — 15,000 couples!

Is It a Moth or a Leaf?

This moth is a master of camouflage. Its wings can even imitate the veins of leaves! And when it lands, it can be as still as a leaf. However, no matter how hard you look, you won't find an *Eacles ormondei* in your backyard. They only live in the forests of Costa Rica.

Pumas Are Formidable Hunters

The puma is a big American feline that pounces on its prey to make it fall. It then kills it by sinking its pointy canines into the back of its prey's neck. Once the puma is satiated, it drags the carcass using its strong jaws and hides it in bushes. This gives the puma a reserve of food for many days.

Tricolored Herons Are Patient

Tricolored herons can stand still for many minutes, waiting for their prey to pass by. When they spot a fish, amphibian, crustacean or even an insect, the herons project their neck forward and catch it with a peck of their beak. This wader from South and Central America rarely misses its prey.

With Tigers, Each Has Its Own Stripes

This feline's fur is unique: the patterns on the coat vary from one to the next and are comparable to our fingerprints. Tigers are never absolutely identical! But their coat serves the same purpose for all: to camouflage the tigers in tall grass so they can surprise their prey.

The Horsefly Is a True Vampire

The female horsefly, like the female mosquito, feeds on warm blood. She gets the blood from humans or animals using her piercing mouthparts. When she stings, she also secretes saliva that can transmit numerous parasites and viruses to her victims.

The Lion's Mark

From this paw print, we can see a lion's back paws and its four digits, contrary to its front paws, which have five. We also see a trace of the paw pads, which allow lions to move silently. However, you won't see any prints left by claws: lions keep them retracted when they're walking.

The Female Hermit Crab's Big Move

This female hermit crab is leaving her shell, which has become too small for her, and moving into a bigger one. She keeps her eggs attached to her until they hatch. The larvae will remain under the maternal shell for many weeks before heading out on their own, to find shelter in the vast ocean.

The Penguin Chick Keeps Warm

Penguin chicks are born in the middle of the Antarctic winter. At birth, they don't yet know how to keep themselves warm nor how to feed themselves. Their father and mother take turns propping them up on their feet, under a fold of skin specifically designed to protect their young. The parent that isn't looking after the chick goes out to sea to eat and bring back food.

Lionesses Take Care of the Meals

It is the female lions that hunt. One or two lionesses pursue the prey, an antelope in this case, and lead it toward the rest of the pride, which hide in tall grass. Once the prey is killed, the males eat first. Lionesses and their cubs must be patient and wait their turn.

This Dragonfly Is in a Precarious Position!

This Central American dragonfly probably mistook this motionless caiman, on which it landed, for a tree stump. Dragonflies like landing on the water's surface in order to surprise insects. Luckily, its swiftness will most likely allow it to avoid being eaten by the caiman.

The Shar-Pei Puppy's Adorable Wrinkles

The skin of this little shar-pei is much too big for him. When he's an adult, he'll have fewer winkles, but his skin will remain pleated. This peculiarity can be useful: if the shar-pei fights with another dog, its loose skin prevents it from being bitten too severly.

The Monk Seal Is Endangered

The monk seal is the only seal that lives in warm waters. It is facing extinction because it only mates on unexplored coasts, which are less and less common. In addition, the female is very skittish and will abandon her baby if a boat or diver approaches. As a result, only an average of one baby out of the two reaches adult age.

Bees See Life in Yellow

In spring and summer, bees collect pollen every morning. They land on flowers, spread the petals, extend their proboscis and aspirate the nectar, which they will transform into honey. Bees also store pollen in "bags" on their back legs. They go from flower to flower and then back to their hive to deposit their treasure.

The White Stork Is Well Traveled

The white stork is a migratory bird that spends its summers in Europe and then flies toward Africa in August. This long trip takes it south of the Sahara and as far as South Africa. At the end of February, the stork leaves these warm regions to find nesting sites in the trees and chimneys of Europe.

The Snowshoe Hare's Changing Colors

Twice a year, the snowshoe hare's fur changes color. It's brown in the summer, to match the colors of the underbrush, and white in winter so it blends in with snow. It's a very useful camouflage that helps it escape from foxes, coyotes and hunters.

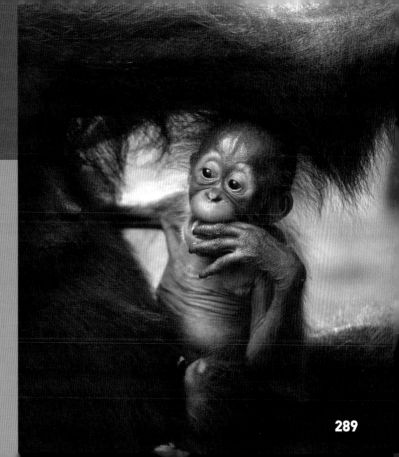

Young Orangutan Imitate Their Parents

This newborn orangutan will stay attached to its mother for more than two years. During that time, it copies the adults' gestures, which helps it learn its group's behaviors: using twigs to catch food, communicating using long, whistling kisses. There are so many gestures, and not all orangutan groups use the same ones.

The Cheetah Is a Formidable Predator

The cheetah is an excellent sprinter: it can reach speeds over 60 miles per hour (100 km/h) over a few hundred feet. Its long legs, supple and muscular body and claws that grip the ground make it the world's fastest terrestrial animal. It's difficult for the gazelles to get away...

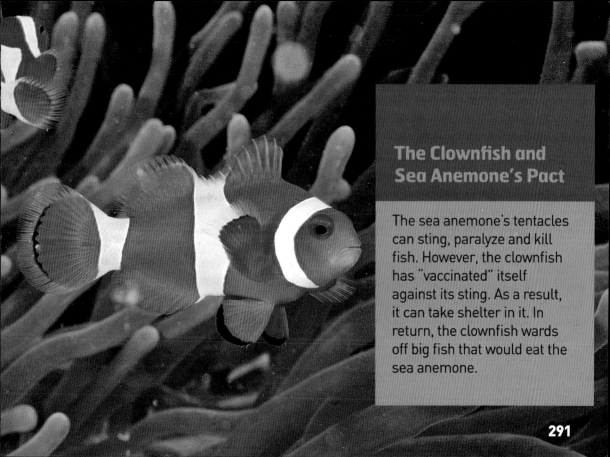

The Clownfish and Sea Anemone's Pact

The sea anemone's tentacles can sting, paralyze and kill fish. However, the clownfish has "vaccinated" itself against its sting. As a result, it can take shelter in it. In return, the clownfish wards off big fish that would eat the sea anemone.

The Llama: A Docile but Touchy Animal

The llama, a mammal from the same family as camels, lives in the Andes. It has been domesticated for many centuries. It is used to carry heavy loads and is also raised for its meat and wool. To defend itself, it spits on whomever dares upset it.

The Wasp Forages — And Devours!

The common wasp, found on all continents, feeds on nectar from certain flowers and on the sweet flesh of ripe fruit. It is also carnivorous. It eats other insects, which it rips apart with its powerful jaw. The wasp then regurgitates this pre-digested food to feed its larvae.

This Baby Black Caiman Is Very Lucky

Female caimans do their best to guard their eggs for three months, but big lizards and mammals often end up eating them, at a rate of 30 eggs per meal. The baby caimans, therefore, have only a small chance of hatching.

The Hazel Dormouse: A Solitary Life

The dormouse leads a solitary and quiet life in the trees. Very comfortable in its surroundings, this rodent can run quickly on or under branches thanks to its paws, which are shaped like hands. In case of danger, it can remain still for several minutes, hooked onto a stem or a leaf.

The Little Chipmunk's Underground Life

The chipmunk nests in the ground. It digs tunnels that can reach more than 11 feet (3.5 m) long, which are linked to a series of rooms that each have a specific purpose: storing debris and excrement, sleeping, storing reserves of grains, fruit and the like for winter or whatever purpose the chipmunk requires.

The Gray Reef Shark: Impressive but Harmless

The gray reef shark, measuring more than 6 feet (2 m) long, often comes out to observe divers. But it's nothing to worry about: it only eats crustaceans and small fish. It's one of the most common sharks of the reefs of the Indian or Pacific Oceans and the Red Sea.

Worm Mush for a Young European Green Woodpecker

Here is a young green wood-pecker being fed its favorite meal of ants that have been partially digested then regurgitated by one of its parents. The parents, who often have five to seven chicks to feed, go back and forth a lot! Luckily, the meals are nourishing, and in three weeks' time the chicks that were bare and blind at birth will become beautiful green woodpeckers ready to fly away.

The Fallow Deer's Outfit

The color of the fallow deer's coat varies depending on its age, its parents' coloring, the place where it lives and the season. Generally, in winter its coat thickens and becomes dark gray to black with brown highlights. Its spots are obviously much less visible then.

The Baby Hare Must Wait

When her baby is born, the female hare places it in the middle of tall grass. The baby stays there, without moving, waiting for the sun to set, when its mother will come to nurse it. The hare seems abandoned, but its mother is never far and keeps an eye on it. If there's any threat, she'll take her baby by the skin of its neck and bring it to safety.

300

The Loggerhead Sea Turtle Is a Drifter

This hatchling will quickly become an expert of marine currents. The loggerhead sea turtle travels a lot, roaming the world's oceans and seas in search of food. The female will also return to the beach where she was born to lay her eggs. The currents are so familiar to them that a loggerhead turtle can fall asleep and drift to its destination.

This Mute Swan Is Ready for Takeoff!

The mute swan is one of the biggest flying birds in the world, which complicates its takeoff. To fly, it needs a large body of water on which to gain speed by running and beating its wings. After this clumsy race, the mute swan gracefully takes flight.

Some Very Playful Wolf Pups

At three weeks old, wolf pups play to practice the hunting techniques they'll put into practice as one-year-olds. They chase each other around, hide and run to get a branch. As adults, they will use this training to catch their prey, but they will also continue to play for the fun of it!

The Rhythm of Icelandic Horses

In addition to the three classic horse gaits — the walk, the trot and the gallop —Icelandic horses have naturally mastered two more. The tölt is a four-beat lateral ambling gait known for its variable speeds, and the "flying pace" is as fast as the gallop but the feet on each side move simultaneously.

The Poison Dart Frog's Mating Rituals

These male and female poison dart frogs, which are found in South and Central America, are looking for the position that will allow them to copulate. The male will place himself in the same direction as the female, on her back. She will then lay her eggs on the base of a leaf, and the male will fertilize them with his semen.

The Very Rare Ethiopian Wolf

Victim of rabies, car traffic and agricultural sprawl, the Ethiopian wolf, which is endemic to Ethiopia, is at risk of disappearing. There are only around 400 of this species remaining. In order to avoid humans, its main enemy, the Ethiopian wolf mostly goes out at night.

This Little Lion Cub Will Become Very Big

Lion cubs are part of a group of lions and lionesses. Its mother, as well as the other lionesses, nurses it for six months. Little by little, the cubs discover their territory and learn how to hunt. At the age of 18 months the young lions are already formidable hunters!

What Is the Purpose of the Butterfly's Wings?

In addition to allowing it to fly, like all insects, butterfly wings capture the sun's energy in the same way as solar panels. The "blood" that flows in the wings is thus heated. This blood, in turn, heats the muscles and the body, allowing these beautiful insects to live and fly.

The Green Tree Python Rests After a Night of Hunting

This python is part of the group of snakes called constrictors. They kill their prey by strangulation, by wrapping themselves around it, before swallowing it whole. Green tree pythons eat mostly at night, feeding on birds or small mammals that live in trees, where they nestle peacefully all day, resting.

309

Never Rub up Against a Flabellina

Flabellinas are a type of mollusk that feed on small animals from the jellyfish family that live on rocks. After swallowing them, the flabellina retrieves the irritating substance they contain and sends it to its spikes. Thus, if a predator tries to eat it, the animal will get stung and will leave the flabellina alone.

The Jackson's Chameleon Is Well Armed

With the three horns on his forehead, this male chameleon looks like a triceratops. In mating season, his horns allow him to fight to attract a female. However, this show doesn't always suffice to seduce a mate. To attract her, the winner must adorn himself with his most beautiful colors, swell his body and proudly raise his horns!

These Cranes Are Gathering Before Their Big Trip

Demoiselle cranes are migratory birds. At the end of fall or beginning of winter, they gather before leaving their nesting area in Central Asia to head toward Sudan and India. In the sky, their flight patterns form either lines or Vs.

The Collared Scops Owl Is Very Small

Collared scops owls are not very big: they measure, on average, just under 6 inches (15 cm). But being small has its advantages. When looking for a nest, these owls of the Indian subcontinent are content with a hole in a tree. They lay their eggs in it, without even adding twigs or grass.

Horseshoe Crabs Landing on the Beach

On full-moon nights at the beginning of summer, beaches along the east coast of America are invaded by horseshoe crabs, prehistoric cousins of spiders and scorpions. They come ashore to mate at low tide, then the female buries her eggs in the sand. A month later, thousands of little horseshoe crabs see the light of day!

The Leopards' Domestic Dispute

In mating season, snow leopards, which are usually solitary, find each other to breed. The male must be patient: if he's too forceful, the female will take out her claws. These acrobatic disputes always end, nonetheless, with mating.

What Are Scales Made Of?

The scales of the Hermann's tortoise's shell are made of keratin, the same material as our nails. They grow regularly, and the visible lines on each of them correspond with growth spurts that are more or less annual, which makes it possible to accurately determine the age of a tortoise within a few years.

The Great Bowerbird's Chivalrous "Trap"

The great bowerbird takes a lot of time to build a beautiful bower made of twigs. It then uses orange and white objects to trace a path leading to it. It's goal? To attract, one after the next, every female in order to mate with her. The females then leave and lay their eggs elsewhere.

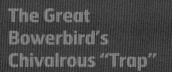

The Brimstone Is Yellow like Butter

Only the male brimstone sports this beautiful color. This species lives all over Europe and is likely the origin of the word "butterfly." More precisely, the word butterfly is actually a contraction of the words "butter colored fly."

The Strawberry and Vanilla Colored Kingsnake

The kingsnakes' coloring normally varies between chocolate brown to black, with yellow, cream or white lines or rings. However, this one is shades of pink! It's because it is "leucistic," meaning its skin is lacking darker pigments. This phenomenon is very rare in these North American snakes.

A Swallow Mother Feeding Her Young

These young barn swallows, hardly out of their nest, are already as big as their mother! Since they don't yet know how to fly correctly, the adults continue to feed them, by regurgitating midges they have swallowed.

The Common Dormouse Is Active from the Moment It Wakes Up

When still barely awake after six months of hibernation, the dormouse begins to build its summer residence. It makes its nest in a bush or a deep tree trunk using foliage and grasses. This animal is very careful: it takes great care to close up the opening of its nest each time it leaves, in order to keep it hidden.

The Black Panther Has the Teeth of a Carnivore

The black panther's mouth is fearsome. Its long, sharp canines close on its prey while its powerful jaws choke it. Then the panther uses its back teeth to cut away pieces of flesh and its rough tongue to tear the last traces of meat from the bones.

The Red-Eyed Tree Frog Is a Bit of a Chameleon

The red-eyed tree frog changes color based on its surroundings: it's green on plants, but on the ground it becomes brown or dark green. When attacked, the frog opens its red eyes wide in the hopes of surprising the predator. It can jump more than 3 feet (1 m) in one hop to get away.

Grizzly Bears Don't Need Fishing Rods

Grizzly bears, which live in the northwest United States and western Canada, have different methods of fishing. Here's one: when salmon go upstream to spawn, they have to jump over waterfalls against the current. Grizzly bears will wait along these waterfalls and catch the jumping salmon in their teeth, and all that's left is to eat them. Simple but efficient!

Toads Are a Gardener's Friend

The common toad lives in forests, ponds and wetlands. It also frequents gardens, where it eats the slugs, snails and other insects that feed on vegetables. In certain regions where toads are numerous, small tunnels are built under roads to ensure they can cross without being crushed.

What Is the Purpose of the the Dik-Dik's Unusual Snout?

The snout of the dik-dik, a small antelope from very warm regions of Africa, contains many veins. When the dik-dik inhales, the blood circulating in its snout cools down, bringing its overall body temperature down. On very hot days, the dik-dik pants like a little dog to allow even more air to circulate.

A Beautiful Orange and Pink Topsnail

This topsnail isn't only a beautiful shell appreciated by collectors and tourists. It's above all an animal, a marine cousin of the land snail, which is killed in order to sell its shell. To protect this animal, we must stop buying these shells!

This Young Silvered Leaf Monkey Doesn't Go Unnoticed

Silvered leaf monkeys are born with a much different coat than their parents. Their rusty orange coloring helps the adults locate them very easily, so they can protect them when needed. The mother is never alone to take care of her baby; the other females babysit.

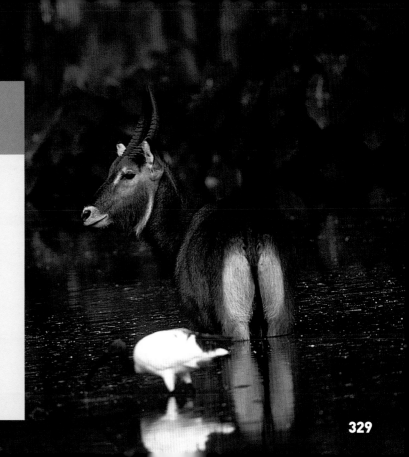

Water: The Waterbuck's Haven

Waterbucks always live near water since they often need to drink. They also take shelter in it when they feel threatened or are followed by a predator that wouldn't dare venture into the water. Their coat, which is covered with oil produced by their skin, helps keep them dry.

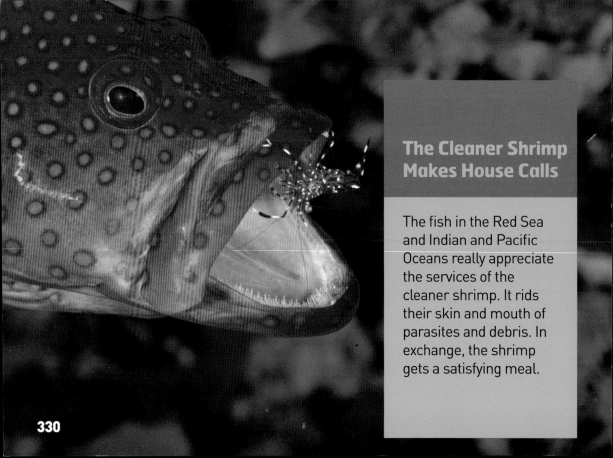

The Cleaner Shrimp Makes House Calls

The fish in the Red Sea and Indian and Pacific Oceans really appreciate the services of the cleaner shrimp. It rids their skin and mouth of parasites and debris. In exchange, the shrimp gets a satisfying meal.

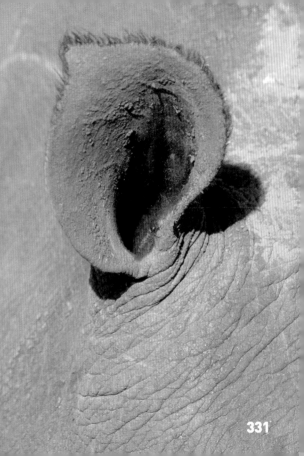

A White Rhinoceros's Beautiful Ear

The white rhinoceroses' ears move toward the direction of sound! Their hearing is exceptional, just like their sense of smell; the white rhinoceros walks with its nose in the air in order to smell the odors of the African savanna. Since their eyesight is very poor, when threatened, the rhino charges blindly, directing itself toward the noise and smell.

Just Born, this Foal Is Already Standing Up

At birth, a foal instinctively knows that it must stand up to nurse. Already standing herself, the mother is tasked with cleaning her baby. In the beginning, the foal is awkward on its long, frail legs. But after only a few days, the foal will begin to distance itself from its mother's warmth to gallop.

This Kitten Already Has Its Little Claws Out

At the tender age of three months, a kitten already knows how to take out its claws. When it's not using them, they are tucked inside its paw pads. A kitten quickly wears down its claws, as it uses them all day long, running after mice and climbing trees, but luckily they grow regularly, just like our nails.

A Young Dromedary

This dromedary calf, which is only a few weeks old, won't stray far from its mother during the first two years of its life. It will nurse for several months before starting to feed on plants. Dromedaries are generally born in the winter, when the temperature is mildest, or during the rainy season, when vegetation is abundant.

334

The Sulfur-Crested Cockatoo's Schedule

In the morning, sulfur-crested cockatoos land on the ground to find food, such as grains, seeds, berries, fruit, larvae and insects. When the tropical heat is too strong, they take shelter in tree foliage. Then, when the freshness of night descends, cockatoos return to the ground to eat.

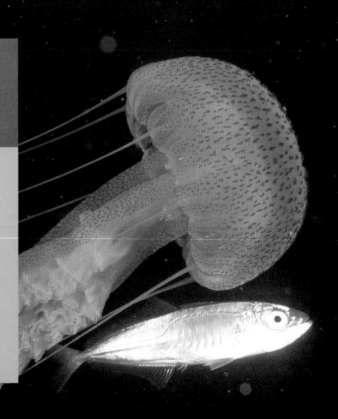

When a Jellyfish and a Fish Are Buddies

This fish has found a surefire way to roam the ocean without the risk of being eaten by a bigger fish: it stays close to a jellyfish. Certain jellyfish in the Indian and Pacific Oceans have a fatal sting. Which inhabitant of the ocean floor would be crazy enough to attack this small fish?

**Lion Cubs:
Still-Fragile
Future Kings**

Their parents might be the kings of the savanna, but these lion cubs are very vulnerable. When the females go hunting, these small felines, even when surrounded by adults who are watching them, can fall victim to a group of hungry hyenas.

The Common Red-Backed Vole's Comfortable Home

Common red-backed voles like to settle into natural shelters like this hallow tree. They make their nest using mosses, grasses and cut up leaves. Their shelter also serves as a pantry, since voles use it to store grains, bark, buds and roots.

The Giant Anteater Pokes Its Nose Everywhere

To find its meal, a giant anteater inserts its tube-shaped snout into termite mounds and anthills. Its long, rough tongue searches the tunnels and comes out covered with insects that it swallows without even chewing. The giant anteater can eat up to 30,000 insects a day, which is how it got the name "anteater."

339

The Gemsbok Is Never Thirsty!

Gemsbok live in desert regions of Africa. They can withstand temperatures over 100°F (40°C) and can go without drinking for several weeks since they eat plants rich in water. During the warmest hours of the day, gemsbok wait in the shade and don't set out to find food until dusk.

The Common Midwife Toad: A Doting Father

The common midwife toad (*Alytes obstetricans*), has a strange way of reproducing: the female lays a string of eggs and transfers them to the male during copulation. From there, he's the only one who protects them and transports them everywhere. When they are ready to hatch, he takes them to a pond.

The Sand Lizard Likes to Sunbathe

After hibernating for up to six months, lizards wake up fresh and relaxed for mating season. Adorned in bright green and having fought some tough battles against other males to attract females, this sand lizard still finds time to warm himself in the sun.

Walruses Like Company

When walruses find themselves on the shore or on Arctic ice, they assemble in groups of up to 100 individuals! These mammals have strong relationships and rely on each other; if a female dies, other females will take in the orphan.

Little Beech Martens Devour Everything!

Beech martens are real athletes and formidable hunters. Fast and flexible, they bounce easily, climb with agility and swim perfectly. They can therefore enjoy a varied menu: birds (here a great spotted woodpecker), mice, eggs, berries and other fruits and insects. They gladly settle in barns and attics in rural areas and sometimes in cities.

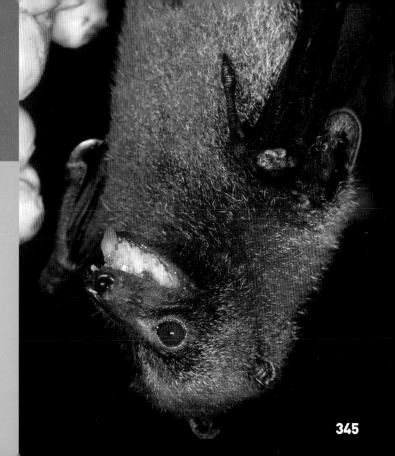

Golden-Capped Fruit Bats Like to Hang Upside Down

Also called giant golden-crowned flying fox, this big bat from Madagascar has powerful claws that allow it to stay suspended from a branch for many hours. They can even eat ripe fruit, pollen and nectar while hanging upside down. This bat's main predator is humans, who hunt it for food.

This Owl Has Radar

Like all nocturnal birds of prey, owls are endowed with an accurate sense of sight that allows them to precisely assess the distance that separates them from their prey. However, their eyes are not very rotatable, so owls must often move their head. Thanks to their extremely flexible neck, their head can almost rotate 360 degrees!

A Cow Tenderly Grooms Her Calf

This cow is cleaning her little one. The calf imitates its mother, which reinforces the family bond between the two animals. Similar licking sessions exist between the adult cows in the heard. The dominant members are groomed by less dominant cows.

The fire salamander is a nocturnal animal. They live in forests, near sources of water where small, slow animals such as snails and slugs can also be found. Since they aren't very fast, fire salamanders can't reasonably go after larger or faster prey for their meals!

Zooming in on a Hedgehog's Quills

To avoid ending up in the belly of a bigger animal, each species has developed its own defense system. Hedgehogs have quills on their back. Thus, when threatened, they roll themselves into a ball, leaving only a bunch of sharp quills exposed to their would-be attacker.

The Crowned Lemur Is on the Trail

This crowned lemur is probably looking for a few small critters or insects to complete its meal, which is mostly made up of vegetation. Like all other Madagascan lemurs, it is extremely agile. Its posterior limbs can propel it over an obstacle measuring almost 10 feet (3 m).

The African Elephant Is a Gentle Giant

African elephants are the largest terrestrial animals — some weigh over 5½ tons (5 metric tons). However, these mammals can run up to 25 miles per hour (40 km/h). Despite their size, they can also delicately walk and move without making a sound, thanks to their feet, which are wrapped in flesh and skin, as though they were built on cushions of air.

351

Mallard Ducks Are Comfortable Everywhere

Mallard ducks will nest on the edges of rivers, lakes, ponds, marshes, urban watering holes — wherever. They can adapt to just about any environment, indifferently eating plants, seeds, insects or small fish. This wild duck is not fussy!

These Common Elands Are Butting Heads

Common elands live in herds of 50 to 100 animals. When conflicts arise, these African antelopes work them out by bashing their horns together. But the battles rarely last long; the weaker of the two animals usually submits to the stronger one before the fighting gets serious. **353**

The Polar Bear's Astonishing Sense of Smell

Polar bears have an acute sense of hearing and a piercing vision. But their sense of smell is most remarkable of all. It allows them to recognize the smell of a beached whale over 12 miles (20 km) away. Once it has found its prey, if the bear is very hungry, it can devour over 110 pounds (50 kg) in one meal!

Cricket or Grasshopper?

We often call any insect that hops a cricket. However, it could also be a grasshopper. But how do you tell them apart? One of the most easily distinguishable differences between the two insects is their antennae. Those of the cricket are as long as their body, while those of the grasshopper are much shorter. This photo is therefore of a grasshopper!

Is this Chimpanzee Deep in Thought?

Chimpanzees are genetically very close to humans. They demonstrate a true intelligence. In nature, they use simple tools such as small branches to extract termites from their nest. In captivity, scientists have conducted experiments to study the chimps' capacity to use language.

The Common Basilisk Is a Lizard That Can Run on Water

Thanks to its slightly webbed digits and very long tail, which helps it stay balanced, the basilisk can run on the water's surface. When threatened, this Central American lizard can also escape by swimming or diving, and it can stay submerged until it feels safe.

The Basking Shark: Terrifying but Harmless

With its length of over 30 feet (10 m) and gaping mouth, it's surprising that the frightening basking shark only swallows marine plankton! This activity occupies it for a large part of spring and summer. Then, when winter comes and plankton is scarce, this giant mysteriously disappears into the ocean's depths.

358

Baby Kangaroos Grow in a Pouch

Kangaroos are a marsupial. They are born blind and hairless, and they continue their postnatal development in their mother's pouch, attached to her teat. The joey stays there over six months and only becomes completely autonomous at the age of one, when it is able to find its own water and food.

The Starfish's Strange Way of Eating

When it captures an oyster, mussel or winkle, a starfish opens it with the help of its five arms covered with hundreds of small suckers. Then, the starfish extracts its stomach from its "mouth" and inserts it into the mollusk. It then re-swallows its stomach once it has digested its prey.

The Harvest Mouse's Circus Act

Barely weighing ¼ ounce (7 grams), the harvest mouse is the smallest rodent. Its featherweight allows it to climb up wheat sheaves without bending them. Using its tail and back legs, it climbs with ease and skill. And it's there, up high in vegetation, that the harvest mouse likes to suspend its nest.

The Little Humpback Whale: A Baby Weighing Over a Ton

The humpback whale is one of 11 species of whale. At birth, they already measure between 14 and 16 feet (4–5 m) and weigh around 1½ tons (1.3 metric tons)! As an adult, this mammal will weigh 33 tons (30 metric tons) and measure 39 to 49 feet (12–15 m) long. Despite its size, this giant of the sea is harmless to humans.

A Young Koala Is Never Without Its Mother!

After spending six months in its mother's pouch, the koala joey stays attached to her back for another six months. During this period, the mother gives her baby eucalyptus leaves that she has already digested to get it used to the food it will be eating in the future. The little one eats this mush, which it retrieves from its mother's anus with its snout.

The Deer's Various Costumes

Deer change their look according to the seasons. In spring, their silky coat is brownish-red and their antlers start to grow. The antlers reach their maximum height in the fall, during mating season. At the beginning of winter, the antlers fall off, and the deer's coat becomes thick and brownish-gray in color.

The Langur's Pirouette

Langurs are acrobatic and playful monkeys, and they are also very good walkers. To find food, they can travel up to 12 miles (20 km) a day. Depending on the region of Asia in which they're found, these monkeys either live in trees or on the ground. They are social animals that are organized in large groups of several dozen individuals.

Hermit Crabs Eat a Bit of Everything!

The hermit crab is a scavenger: it eats plant debris and dead animals as well as small live prey. This voracious crustacean adapts its diet according to the area in which it's living. It iss found in seas and oceans around the world.

A Skewer of Little Bee-Eaters?

Little bee-eaters are not solitary animals. They are always seen in couples or in families. They catch insects mid-flight, and if it's a wasp or a bee, the bee-eater hits in on a branch to detach the stinger to ensure it doesn't get stung when it swallows it.

The Lusitano Is a Skilled Stuntman

Thanks to their good balance and great response to handling, Lusitanos have long been considered the perfect breed of warhorse. Today, this Portuguese horse is highly sought after for film and television and for equestrian races.

The Bald Eagle: An American Symbol

Since 1970, to save the bald eagle, the use of certain electrical lines has been restricted and certain pesticides have been prohibited. The use of lead in bullets has also been eliminated. Lead is toxic to birds of prey, which ingest the metal when they eat birds injured or killed by hunters.

The Shovel-Snouted Lizard's "Thermal Dance"

In the Namib Desert of Africa, the shovel-snouted lizard dances strangely: it lifts its legs one after the other in order to cool them down. And then, balanced on the ends of its feet, it goes out searching for food, maintaining the minimum of contact with the burning-hot sand.

PHOTO CREDITS

pp. 2: C. Ruoso, pp 3 t: Klein et Hubert [Bios], pp 3 b: M. Harvey [Bios]

Bios: pp. 5: M. Duhau, pp. 9: A. Torterotot, pp. 11: P. Kobeh, pp. 12: M. Harvey, pp. 13: J.-M. Prevot, pp. 14: J.-L. Zimermann, pp. 18: M. Harvey, pp. 24: M. et C. Denis-Huot, pp. 25: J. Herras, pp. 29: D. Bringard, pp. 30: D. Heuclin, pp. 31: M. Harvey, pp. 32: J.-C. Vincent, pp. 34: Gayo, pp. 38: Klein et Hubert, pp. 41: Maywald/Fotonatura, pp. 47: J. Dragesco, pp. 51: P. Henry, pp. 52: P. Sabonnadière, pp. 54: J.-J. Alcalay, pp. 56: J.-C. Vincent, pp. 58: T. Allofs, pp. 59: M. Harvey, pp. 63: N. Dennis, pp. 64: J.-J. Alcalay, pp. 67: J.-J. Alcalay, pp. 71: Klein et Hubert, pp. 75: R. Valarcher, pp. 79: D. Heuclin, pp. 83: Stoelwinder Fotografie, pp. 87: T. Allofs, pp. 89: J.-J. Alcalay, pp. 91: Klein et Hubert, pp. 93: B. Cole, pp. 94: Klein et Hubert, pp. 96: X. Eichaker, pp. 97: F. Bruemmer, pp. 102: B. Fischer, pp. 103: D. Heuclin, pp. 106: M. Rauch, pp. 110: M. Ribette, pp. 113: T. Allofs, pp. 120: Klein et Hubert, pp. 121: J. Cancalosi, pp. 123: M. Duhau, pp. 127: F. Bavendam, pp. 138: M. Gunther, pp. 140: C. Ruoso, pp. 149: R. Valarcher, pp. 150: J. Denis Nigel, pp. 153: H. Hall/OSF, pp. 154: J. Herras, pp. 157: Klein et Hubert, pp. 158: J.-C. Vincent, pp. 164: T. Allofs, pp. 165: R. Dirschertl, pp. 171: D. Watts, pp. 175: J. Rotman, pp. 176: J. Dragesco, pp. 178: Klein et Hubert, 0pp. 184: F. Mordel, pp. 188: B. Cole, pp. 191: Klein et Hubert, pp. 196: M. Gunther, pp. 203: Mafart-Renodier, pp. 219: Franco/Bonnard, pp. 224: Denis-Huot, pp. 227: G. Bily, pp. 229: P. Vernay, pp. 239: D. Delfino, pp. 242: G. Schulz, pp. 243: G. Nicolet, pp. 245: Mafart-Renodier, pp. 247: M. et C. Denis-Huot, pp. 249: R. Henno/Wildelife pictures, pp. 250: F. Pawlowski, pp. 251: M. Harvey, pp. 252: C. Migeon, pp. 253: P. Weimann, pp. 254: C. Sams-P. Arnold, pp. 256: Denis-Huot, pp. 257: R. Le Guen, pp. 260: R. Cavaignaux, pp. 269: M. Harvey, pp. 273: M. et C. Denis-Huot, pp. 274: Y. Thonnerieux, pp. 275: Klein et Hubert, pp. 277: F. Savigny, pp. 279: R. de la Harpe, pp. 282: Harvey, pp. 285: Di Dominico/Panda Photo, pp. 292: L. Mike, pp. 294: T. Montford, pp. 295: J.-L. Zimermann, pp. 297: J.-C. Robert, pp. 298: F. Fève, pp. 301: M. Gunther, pp. 303: Klein et Hubert, pp. 306: M. Gunther, pp. 307: Denis-Huot, pp. 308: T. Da Cunha, pp. 310: J. Rotman, pp. 314: J.- P. Sylvestre, pp. 318: J. Herras, pp. 327: B. Brandon, pp. 342: B. Fischer, pp. 347: C. Ruoso, pp. 348: B. Fischer, pp. 321: B. Lundberg, pp. 330: P. Kobeh, pp. 332: Klein et Hubert, pp. 336: F. Pacorel, pp. 338: F. Fève, pp. 339: T. Allofs, pp. 340: Klein et Hubert, pp. 344: R. Cavaignaux, pp. 345: M. Harvey, pp. 350: M. Harvey, pp. 351: M. et C. Denis-Huot, pp. 354: Klein et Hubert, pp. 360: Secret Sea Visions/P. Arnold, pp. 361: M. Powles/Still pictures, pp. 362: B. Brandon, pp. 363: Klein et Hubert, pp. 367: M. Harvey, pp. 369: T. Allofs, pp. 370: M. Harvey

Boiselle: pp. 10: M. Idersson, pp. 210: G. Boiselle, pp. 304: G. Boiselle, pp. 368: C. Slawik

Cogis: pp. 15: Dubois, pp. 21: Gissey, pp. 33: DHF, pp. 36: Gissey, pp. 37: Gissey, pp. 42: Lili, pp. 44: Dubois, pp. 46: Nicaise, pp. 48: Fagot, pp. 53: Bernie, pp. 60: Bernie, pp. 65: Lanceau, pp. 72: Gissey, pp. 86: Varin, pp. 88: Gissey, pp. 107: Dubios, pp. 115: Varin, pp. 116: Gissey, pp. 117: Gissey, pp. 119: Gissey, pp. 128: Lili, pp. 129: Nicerise, pp. 130: Gissey, pp. 132: Gissey, pp. 133: Gissey, pp. 177: Gissey, pp. 199: Varin, pp. 208: Lili, pp. 209: Lanceau, pp. 218: Dufresne, pp. 220: Gissey, pp. 221: Gissey, pp. 234: Lili, pp. 241: Gissey, pp. 255: Gissey, pp. 258: Gissey, pp. 284: Lanceau, pp. 296: Dubois, pp. 319: I. Français, pp. 326: Gissey, pp. 329: Varin, pp. 333: Dufresne, pp. 334: Gissey, pp. 352: Gissey, pp. 353: Varin, pp. 359: Fagot, pp. 364: Gissey, pp. 366: Français

Colibri: pp. 5: J.-L. Paumard

Fotonatura: pp. 155: M. Harvey, pp. 322: Kimball

Grunewald: pp. 81, pp. 90, pp. 131, pp. 166, pp. 183, pp. 235

Hoa Qui: pp. 16: M. Denis-Huot, pp. 17: K. Guermoud, pp. 151: M. Denis-Huot, pp. 190: P. de Wilde, pp. 222: Photobank Yokohama, pp. 223: A. Fuchs

Hoaqui/Age footstockz: pp. 40: C. Monteath, pp. 68: M. Breuer, pp. 104: J. Milchanowski, pp. 181: F. Poelking, pp. 197: J. A. Jiménez, pp. 266: J. Milchanowski, pp. 267: S. Grover, pp. 270: W. Bollmann, pp. 287: K. Schafer, pp. 324: M. Newman, pp. 331: W. Bollmann, pp. 341: B. Borrell, pp. 355: R. Campillo

Jacana: pp. 6: Y. Gladu, pp. 28: P. de Wilde, pp. 76: M. Danegger, pp. 78: T. Walker, pp. 122: C. Jouan – J. Rius, pp. 125: C. Jouan – J. Rius, pp. 135: S. Cordier, pp. 136: A. Et M. Shah, pp. 147: T. Walker, pp. 161: Doc White/NPL, pp. 163: P. Lorne, pp. 174: I. Arndt, pp. 189: E. A. Soder, pp. 195: Lynn Stone/NPL, pp. 198: Dupont/Delorme, pp. 202: M. Danegger, pp. 204: Rouxaime, pp. 213: P. Lorne, pp. 217: A. Shah, pp. 226: P. Lorne, pp. 230: I. Arndt, pp. 232: M. Luquet, pp. 236: C. Lotscher, pp. 261: D. et S. Balfour, pp. 265: P. Louisy/Grandeur nature, pp. 272: S. Cordier, pp. 278: Chris Martin Bahr, pp. 286: P. Lorne, pp. 293: Rouxaime, pp. 323: S. Cordier, pp. 343: S. Cordier, pp. 349: H. Schwind

Jacana /Nature PL: pp. 62: D. Nill, pp. 143: G. Douwma, pp. 182: A. Cooper, pp. 263: P. Oxford, pp. 264: R. Du Toit, pp. 325: I. Arndt

NOAA Fisheries Service: pp. 358: Greg Skomal

Phone: pp. 19: J.-M. Labat, pp. 22: P. Danna, pp. 45: J. -P. Ferrero, pp. 61: V. Munier, pp. 74: P. Danna, pp. 82: S. Cordier, pp. 95: S. Corider, pp. 108: F. Gohier, pp. 109: J. -P. Ferrero, pp. 118: P. Danna, pp. 126: J.-M. Labat, pp. 167: T. Aichinger/Visual and Written, pp. 168: F. Gohier, pp. 170: T. Aichinger/Visual and Written, pp. 172: R. Valter, pp. 185: J.-M. Labat, pp. 193: Ferrero/Labat, pp. 200: J.-M. Labat, pp. 215: Cordier, pp. 216: M. Gosalvez/Visual and Written, pp. 228: Hellio/Van Ingen, pp. 262: O. Villa, pp. 281: G. Robertson, pp. 299: P. Danna, pp. 300: J. Sierra

Photononstop: pp. 8: IFA, pp. 20: B. Coleman, pp. 26: F. Gilson, pp. 39: B. Coleman, pp. 50: IFA, pp. 57: IFA, pp. 77: IFA, pp. 80: IFA, pp. 92: IFA, pp. 99: B. Coleman, pp. 101: IFA, pp. 105: Simeone, pp. 111: IFA, pp. 112: B. Coleman, pp. 124: IFA, pp. 134: B. Coleman, pp. 142: IFA, pp. 145: IFA, pp. 146: B. Coleman, pp. 156: IFA, pp. 159: IFA, pp. 169: B. Coleman, pp. 173: IFA, pp. 179: IFA, pp. 186: B. Coleman, pp. 201: IFA, pp. 205: B. Coleman, pp. 212: IFA, pp. 214: IFA, pp. 237: IFA, pp. 240: IFA, pp. 244: IFA, pp. 246: B. Coleman, pp. 248: IFA, pp. 271: B. Coleman, pp. 276: IFA, pp. 280: B. Coleman, pp. 283: B. Coleman, pp. 291: J. -C.-D. Pratt, pp. 302: IFA, pp. 305: IFA, pp. 309: A. Even, pp. 311: IFA, pp. 316: IFA, pp. 337: B. Coleman, pp. 346: IFA

Rapho: pp. 141: J.-L. Manaud

C. Ruoso: pp. 23, pp. 27, pp. 35, pp. 43, pp. 49, pp. 55, pp. 66, pp. 69, pp. 70, pp. 85, pp. 98, pp. 100, pp. 114, pp. 137, pp. 139, pp. 152, pp. 160, pp. 180, pp. 187, pp. 192, pp. 207, pp. 231, pp. 238, pp. 259, pp. 289, pp. 312, pp. 313, pp. 315, pp. 317, pp. 320, pp. 328, pp. 335, pp. 365

Stock image: pp. 162, pp. 225

Sunset: pp. 357: NPHA

INDEX

A

African buffaloes, 33
African elephants, 87, 351
albatrosses, sooty, 250
Albert's squirrels, 144
alligators, 39, 112
alpine ibexes, 192
American white pelicans, 61
anemones, sea, 291
anteaters, 339
ants, 163, 204, 213
Apollo butterflies, 72
arctic foxes, 78, 135
argiope spiders, 189
armadillos, 108, 272
Asian elephants, 228
Atlantic puffins, 227
Australian short-necked turtles, 139
azure damselflies, 32

B

baboons, 85, 136, 251
Baird's tapirs, 99
bald eagles, 369
barbary macaques, 70
barnacles, 188
barn owls, 110
barn swallows, 320
basilisks, common, 357
basking sharks, 358
bats, 57, 345
bears, 38, 51, 120, 126, 206, 324, 354
beech martens, 344
bees, 25, 101, 286
beetles, 23, 88, 106, 116, 141, 222, 241, 258
belugas, 161
bison, 266
black-backed jackals, 269
black caimans, 294
black-headed gulls, 198
black leopards, 215
black panthers, 215, 322
blennies, 17
blue-and-yellow macaws, 42
blue peacocks, 64
bluespotted ribbontail stingrays, 265
blue tits, 52
boars, wild, 179, 225
boas, Madagascar, 43
bobcats, 94
bonobos, 160
boring clams, 143
bottlenose dolphins, 223
boxer crabs, 167
Brazilian tapirs, 169
brimstones, 318
brown bears, 51, 126
buffaloes, 33
buff-tailed bumblebees, 25
bush vipers, 243
butterflies, 56, 72, 308, 318

C

caimans, 112, 230, 294
camels, 138
camouflage methods, 50, 74, 244, 274, 277
Cape ground squirrels, 54
capuchins, white-headed, 37
capybaras, 164
caracaras, 164
caterpillars, 158, 238
cats, 47, 208, 333
    see also individual names of big cats
centipedes, 13
Central American dragonflies, 283
chameleons, 12, 244, 311
chamois, 75
cheetahs, 24, 290
chimpanzees, 66, 356
chipmunks, 296
cicadas, 154
clams, 143
clownfish, 291
cockatoos, sulfur crested, 335
coconut crab, 18
coleopteran beetles, 222

collared scops owls, 313
corrals, 93
cows, 347
coypus, 53
crabeater seals, 123
crabs, 18, 69, 194, 216, 280, 314, 366
cranes, 131, 312
crickets, 177, 214
crinoids, 22
crocodiles, 59, 67
crowned lemurs, 350

D
damselflies, azure, 32
deer, 180, 184, 201, 248, 299, 364
demoiselle cranes, 312
desmans, 30
dik-diks, 326
dogs, 86, 284
dolphins, bottlenose, 223
donkeys, 157
dormice, 295, 321
dragonets, 146
dragonflies, 130, 181, 197, 283
dromedaries, 138, 334
ducks, mallard, 352

E
Eacles ormondei, 274

eagles, 183, 369
eared seals, 178
egrets, great, 80
elands, common, 353
elephants, 87, 193, 228, 351
emperor moths, 65
emperor tamarins, 117
emus, 20
Ethiopian wolves, 306
Eurasian blue tits, 52
Eurasian lynxes, 258, 259
European fire ants, 204
European green woodpeckers, 212, 298
European plaices, 205
European rabbits, 187

F
fallow deer, 299
fawns, 248
fennecs, 221
fire salamanders, 348
flabellinas, 310
flamingoes, 268, 273
flickers, 124
foals, 332
foxes, 78, 135, 147, 182, 221, 345
fox squirrels, 107
Friesian horses, 210
frigatebirds, 5

frilled-neck lizards, 203
frogs, 34, 77, 305, 323

G
gannets, Northern, 134, 246
geckoes, 81
geese, 105
gemsboks, 340
genets, 209
gentoo penguins, 233
German shepherds, 86
ghost crabs, 69
giant anteaters, 339
gibbons, white-handed, 115
giraffes, 247, 270
golden-capped fruit bats, 345
golden marmosets, 91
goose barnacles, 188
gorillas, 31, 46
goshawks, 237
grasshoppers, 355
gray reef sharks, 297
great bowerbirds, 317
great egrets, 80
greater flamingoes, 273
greater kudus, 235
great hornbills, 35
green herons, 48
green iguanas, 190

green lizards, 21
green tree pythons, 309
green woodpeckers, 298
grey langurs, 98
grizzly bears, 324
groundhogs, 15
gulls, black-headed, 198

H
hares, 142, 288, 300
hartebeests, 125
harvester ants, 213
harvest mice, 361
hawks, 242, 262
Hazel dormice, 295
hedgehogs, 62, 220, 349
Hermann's tortoises, 156, 316
hermit crabs, 280, 366
herons, 48, 80, 276
hippopotamuses, 114, 148, 217
hooded seals, 97
hornbills, great, 35
hornets, 92
horses, 10, 210, 304, 332, 368
horseshoe crabs, 314
humpback whales, 362
hyacinth macaws, 199
hyenas, 19, 122

I
ibexes, 192
Icelandic horses, 304

iguanas, 190
impalas, 162, 264

J
jackals, 269
Jackson's chameleons, 244, 311
jaguars, 58, 84, 145
Japanese cranes, 131
Japanese macaques, 109
jays, 44
jellyfish, 60, 336
jerboas, 176

K
kangaroos, 100, 140, 359
kingfishers, 14
king penguins, 113
kingsnakes, 319
kittens, 333
koalas, 73, 363
komodo dragons, 137
krill, 45, 89
kudus, 235

L
ladybugs, 226
langurs, 98, 365
leaf beetles, 23
lemurs, 155, 245, 350
leopards, 55, 195, 215, 315
Lilian's lovebirds, 191
lions, 256, 279, 282, 307, 337

little bee-eaters, 367
little egrets, 254
lizards, 21, 96, 137, 342, 370
llamas, 292
loggerhead sea turtles, 301
long-tailed weasels, 104
lovebirds, Lillian's, 191
Lusitanos horses, 368
lynxes, 231, 259

M
macaques, 70, 109
macaws, 42, 199
Madagascar boas, 43
mallard ducks, 352
manatees, West Indian, 249
mandarinfish, 146
mandarins, 128
mandrills, 85
marmosets, 91
martens, 344
meerkats, 150
mice, 260, 295, 321, 361
millipedes, 49
minotaur beetles, 106
moles, 30
monkeys. silvered leaf, 328
monk seals, 285
moths, 65, 274
mouflons, 149
mountain gorillas, 46
mudskippers, 27

muskrats, 132

N
North American harvester ants, 213
North American porcupines, 236
North American prairie dogs, 234
Northern gannets, 134, 246
Northern goshawks, 237
nutrias, 53

O
ocelots, 168
octopuses, 175, 186
okapis, 129
orangutans, 218, 289
ostriches, 95, 151
otters, 8
owls, 110, 219, 313, 346
oxpeckers, red-billed, 264

P
pandas, 200, 206
pangolins, 63
panther chameleons, 12
panthers, 7, 215, 322
paper wasps, 36
parasites, 23
patato beetles, 116
peacock, 64
pelicans, 61, 207
penguins, 9, 113, 233, 281
Peringuey's adders, 90

pigs, 196
plaices, European, 205
plants, carnivorous, 79
poison dart frogs, 34, 305
polar bears, 38, 120, 354
porcupines, 236
prairie dogs, 234
prairie rattlesnakes, 103
praying mantis, 121
pufferfish, 211
puffins, 227
pumas, 275
puss moth caterpillars, 158
pygmy hippopotamus, 114
pythons, green tree, 309

R
rabbits, European, 187
raccoons, 68
rattlesnakes, 103
red-billed oxpeckers, 264
red deer, 201
red-eyed tree frogs, 323
red pandas, 200
red pouch displays, 5
red rock crabs, 194
redshanks, common, 83
rhinoceros beetles, 88
rhinoceroses, 16, 331
right whales, 89
ring-tailed lemurs, 245
roosters, 239

S
salamanders, fire, 348
sand cats, 47
sandfish, 96
sand lizards, 342
scallops, 252
scarab beetles, 141
scorpions, 174
sea anemones, 11, 291
seabed animals, 93
sea hawks, 242
seahorses, 74
sea lilies, 22
seals, 6, 28, 97, 123, 178, 240, 285
sea stars, 127, 360
sea turtles, 257, 301
sharks, 297, 358
Shar-Peis, 284
sheep, 40, 202
shells, 127
Shire horses, 10
shovel-snouted lizards, 370
shrews, 255
shrikes, 102
shrimps, cleaner, 330
Siamese cats, 208
Siamese fighting fish, 29
silvered leaf monkeys, 328
skinks, 96
sloths, two-toed, 133
small emperor moths, 65
snails, 127, 267, 271, 327

snakes, 43, 90, 103, 243, 319
snow leopards, 55, 195, 315
snow monkeys, 109
snowshoe hares, 288
sooty albatrosses, 250
southern masked weavers, 173
southern right whales, 89
Spanish dancers, 165
sperm whales, 153
spider crabs, 216
spiders, 111, 189, 232, 263
spike-topped apple snails, 271
sponges, 93
spotted hyenas, 19, 122
squirrels, 54, 107, 144
stag beetles, 241
stags, 180
stalked barnacles, 188
starfish, 127, 360
Stellar's jay, 44
Steller's sea eagles, 183
stick-insects, 152
stingrays, bluespotted ribbontail, 265
storks, white, 159, 287
sulfur crested cockatoos, 335
swallows, barn, 320
swallowtail butterflies, 56
swallowtail caterpillars, 238
swans, mute, 302
sweetlips, 118

T
tamarins, emperor, 117
tapirs, 99, 169
tarantulas, 232, 263
tigers, 41, 253, 277
tits, Eurasian blue, 52
toads, 325, 341
topsnails, 327
tortoises, Hermann's, 156, 316
toucans, keel-billed, 71
tricolored herons, 276
triplefins, tropical striped, 170
turtles, 139, 257, 301
two-toed sloths, 133

V
Verreaux's Sifakas, 155
vipers, 103, 243
voles, common red-backed, 338

W
walruses, 172, 343
warthogs, 261
wasps, 36, 293
waterbucks, 329
weasels, 76, 104, 209
weavers, southern masked, 173
western gray kangaroos, 140
West Indian manatees, 249
whales, 89, 153, 161, 362

white-handed gibbons, 115
white-headed capuchin, 37
white-nosed coatis, 119
white rhinoceroses, 16, 331
white storks, 159, 287
white tigers, 253
whooper swans, 166
wild boars, 179, 225
wildebeests, 185
wolf spiders, 111
wolverines, 82
wolves, 26, 229, 303, 306
wombats, 171
wood mice, 260
woodpeckers, 212, 298

Z
zebras, 224